Thank you for your

1

Best
P. 28Neill

2

UNINVITED GUESTS

(The cloud of Alzheimer's disease)

By

Gayle Lunning

ISBN 13 978-1723514111
ISBN 10 172351411X
Copyright Gayle Lunning 2016

Cover Design by

Jessica Scott
Uniquely Tailored.com

Forward

To see objects, people, apparitions or the like, is not unusual for the unfortunate suffering from early onset Alzheimer's. It happened to my best friend and is now happening to my sister. What is very real to them is a great source of concern for their immediate and extended families. In our parents childhood, and earlier generations, often is heard, "Grandpa is getting senile." when explaining his (or her) forgetfulness. Dementia or Alzheimer's were unfamiliar terms or conditions.

In the early or mild stages of Alzheimer's disease, one may become confused when in familiar places. A street, a park, or store may suddenly seem foreign. Items in the grocery store previously located at will, are now difficult to find and the individual blames the store for moving things around. When attempting to pay for the items finally located, the afflicted find themselves fumbling with cash to make the purchase, sometimes even handing the 'wad' of cash to the cashier to expedite the transaction. The unfortunate victim finds it hard to complete tasks that previously had been menial and readily accomplished. They may not tie shoes, or button shirts, as deftly as they once had. Their personality takes a shift; some become negative, others argumentative, while most become pensive or withdrawn. The mild stage finds them often losing or misplacing things. After an extensive search, I recently found my car keys in my left hand pants pocket instead of the right hand pocket where I usually place them. Does that mean I am in the early stages? I suspect we all have lapses in memory such as that, but at the onset of Alzheimer's this phenomena occurs persistently.

The mid or moderate stage finds increased memory loss and confusion. People that are well known have suddenly become nameless. There usually is recognition, but placing a name with the familiar face is a laboriously lengthy task, if accomplished at all. This is not limited to infrequent acquaintances but unfortunately, extends to family members and friends. In this stage of moderate Alzheimer's, one may seem relatively normal but often in the company of friends or relatives they struggle to recall a name. The understanding friend or family member will laugh at a story related a short time ago to avoid embarrassing a friend. Tasks with multiple steps are hard to complete and frequently some of the steps are left out. Imagine a favorite recipe with a key ingredient missing. Personal hygiene, grooming and appearance are no longer important to one that has always taken pride in their personal presentation.

The severe or latter stages of this dreaded dementia finds the afflicted unable to recognize family or friends. Perhaps only a select fortunate few are recognized by name or facial expression. The disheartened close family member greeted with a blank stare, or fearful look in the patient's eye, faces the realization that Alzheimer's is closing off the mind completely. The patient is often no longer able to communicate other than by grunting, groaning or moaning. Assistance with all activities associated with daily living is required and they begin to drool and lose control of bladder and bowel functions. Too soon the ultimate end of Alzheimer's is... death.

How does one cope with losing a close friend or relative to Alzheimer's disease? The signs signaling the onset of the disease are usually there to recognize, but too often ignored as we pass our friends or loved ones off as just being 'forgetful'. I did when my best friend began the descent into the dreaded fog of Alzheimer's. Being separated by nearly five hundred miles and relying on telephone conversations every other month, I was not aware of his mood swings or change in personality. Frequently I suspect minor changes are ignored as the normal progression of aging. Should I have known it was Alzheimer's coming on when he looked so atypical at his wife's funeral? Slumped forward in the front pew, he stared blankly at me as I delivered a eulogy for his wife. He did not exhibit what I considered a normal emotion for the loss of a loved one. But then "Rick" was a very strong man. I admired his strength of character and it was something I, and many of his close friends, found we could lean on in our times of trouble. I considered his emotionless expression highly unusual, but then...

When he called a couple weeks later to tell me of the ghosts he was seeing, that should have raised a flag of great concern. After the phone call, I was perplexed but passed it off as grief from having lost his beloved. When I visited to 'see' his ghosts, I tried to advise him to see a doctor but Rick was a strong, proud man and adamantly declined.

A flag was raised among family members when my sister reported seeing and hearing a stalker outside her country home. Initially, great concern was raised as she lived alone and perhaps susceptible to a stalker preying on widowed or single women. Our concern included support for the purchase of a pistol and surveillance cameras for protection. The family's concern shifted when after several months of 'visits' by her stalker failed to be detected by surveillance. The perseverance of the purported stalker eventually led to an undesirable realization by a family reluctant to confront her with our suspicions.

My 'best bud' Rick, told me he retired early because he could not remember why he called a sales meeting. (an indication of the moderate stage, increased memory loss and confusion.) He had to let someone else conduct the meeting as he forgot what it concerned. Unable to see the forest for the trees I made the flippant remark; "Aw Rick, It's just Al Heimer coming to get you." How often, I have been tormented by those words. How often, do I wish I had been aware of and able to recognize the signs. Perhaps a doctor could not have prevented, or slowed down, the onset of his disease, but… if only I had demanded…

Some other signs of the moderate stage of Alzheimer's; problems recognizing friends or family, difficulty with tasks having multiple steps or a lack of concern for personal hygiene and appearance were not apparent with "Rick". He was always a 'natty' dresser and capable of multitasking, or so I thought.

Even in the later stages he was able to recognize family and some friends but could not recall having seen them just recently. His daughter told me of a visit where she had to leave him briefly to go to the store, and upon her return, he did not realize she had been there only minutes earlier. He was able to communicate and was not moaning and groaning but did need assistance with all activities of daily living. His personality changed dramatically during the latter stages as he became more belligerent, yet also withdrawn. Near the end, he lost control of bodily functions which is extremely painful to the pride of such a strong man.

The funeral for my best friend, for my brother by other parents, was emotional for me. Could I have helped him? Can I help my sister? Do we not know of someone now battling Alzheimer's? Do we not wish there is something we can do to help? Perhaps somewhere, someday, someone will unlock the mystery that shrouds those afflicted and if not cure, at least prevent the uninvited from entering.

TABLE OF CONTENTS

Chapter One...................................13
Chapter Two..................................19
Chapter Three...............................29
Chapter Four.................................45
Chapter Five..................................60
Chapter Six...................................68
Chapter Seven..............................73
Chapter Eight................................80
Chapter Nine.................................96
Chapter Ten..................................105
Chapter Eleven.............................119
Chapter Twelve.............................129
Chapter Thirteen...........................138
Chapter Fourteen..........................152
Chapter Fifteen..............................164
Chapter Sixteen.............................176
Chapter Seventeen.......................182
Chapter Eighteen...........................197

Chapter One

OK! So just what is a ghost?

We can eliminate Casper, or can we? Are they dressed in sheets like we see on Halloween? Are they the frightening wispy cloud monsters depicted in movies? I really want to know because what I see is nothing like the comic books or movies. Yes, you heard me, what I see.

At times they have sheets over their head, hmmm... I guess more like pillowcases than sheets. And there are holes cut in them for the eyes, well, not really cut, but... just there. They usually sit on the couch in my bedroom and ignore me when I come in, or try to talk to them. They don't answer me. How rude. HA HA! (At least I can laugh about it now.)

Sometimes they float about above my ceiling fan, not keeping time with the fan, just... hovering around the blades. Perhaps they are curious, or playing some dangerous game with the fan. Wait... dangerous? Can they be hurt? Will they get the stuffing knocked out of them? (There I go, making a funny again.) And here's another thing: I have never seen them eat. My food is undisturbed. I have never seen them go to the bathroom, or wash themselves. They just sit or 'flit' about. And how do they get into my house? They don't open doors. Maybe they come through the window beside my bed, but I never see the curtains move.

The "pillowcases" are not transparent, or white, or any particular color. Their color changes with the time of day. None of the colors are bright, all somewhat dull, more grayish as if washed out. One of them was in bed with me and she... I'm pretty sure it was a she... good grief, I hope it was a she... OK, I don't want to be in bed with a 'he' so, yes... she... was in a purple covering. She was looking at me and I had to turn away for fear I might think about being unfaithful to Kay.

But most of the time I see them without "pillowcases" and have been able to see their features, albeit not clearly. When I am able to see their features, none of them strike a familiar chord. They are quite thin, although the women, I think, are somewhat attractive. If they resembled someone I know that has passed on I would call them by name to elicit a response. No, they just sit there. I talk to them, but they do not answer.

"Hello." Nothing. "Can I help you?" I lean slightly forward, my hands outstretched. **"Do you want something? Can I get you anything?"** I almost shouted.

No response. They appear to look at me, but do they see me? They move, or at least appear to move. It's more of a shimmering or vibrating movement. Their eyes move a little, but I can't tell for sure... whoa, there is something about those eyes. They are always looking at me. No matter where I go, the eyes follow me. What was that movie where the eyes in the picture on the staircase always followed the hero? (Or was he a villain?) Now I am the hero being watched and the eyes follow me, especially by one male that is there whenever my

14

uninvited guests show up. He looks at me sinister like and... OK, I'll admit it, he gives me the creeps.

At first I thought they were small people, these ghosts or whatever, but I soon realized they have no legs. Did they have legs when I first saw them, and did not notice that slight deformity? Yes, they are much smaller in stature than normal people. They just sit on the couch pillows and their lower bodies are kind of... well... fuzzy.

It was just after dark the first time I saw them. How long has it been, a week, two weeks? I don't remember how long. I came in from the patio, threw away my empty beer cans, and headed into my bedroom; there they were, sitting on my couch by the window. I stopped abruptly about fifteen feet away, mouth open and eyes wide, stunned. My blood turned cold, my knees weak and my heart began to pound. A loud ringing rose in my ears, my hands tingling and the hair standing up on the back on my neck. Turning to run quickly, my shoulder struck the doorjamb as I fled, stumbling to the bedroom across the hall fighting to maintain my balance, certain they would pounce on me if I fell.

Gaining the safety of the guest bedroom, I am breathing heavily as I press the lock on the door behind me. Only blankets in a state of disarray, no sheets, are on the bed, I hurriedly jam the bed against the door and stand staring at the entrance. Standing behind the bed for several minutes, I try to comprehend what I saw. My chest is rising and my breath labored as I press my hand to my forehead. How many times have I watched movies where

15

these "things" tear someone from limb to limb? Am I in danger?

Trembling and cold, I hold out my hand. There are tremors in my chest and arms, my hand shakes vigorously. Flexing my fingers, I stare at my hand. There is no sensation of movement, although the fingers open and close. I am not easily frightened but this...what is this? What did I see? I am no longer sure.

Listening intently, I try to detect the slightest movement or sound in the house; I am not alone; that much I am sure of. But who, or what, is with me? Could it simply be some light coming off the golf course? Or moonlight reflecting off the television? The television in the master bedroom is not on, so it could not be a reflection from a TV program.

Wait! What did I just hear? What was that sound? Creaking? Someone, or something is coming. A high pitched, but low volume, whine, not a screech but... oh God! No, no, it's OK, just the ringing in my ears... I think. There is also the heavy pounding of my heart in my chest. I feel, and almost hear, every beat of my heart as if it were about to jump out of my chest. Shallow breathing comes rapidly through my open mouth.

What was that? What was that noise? Oh my God! Am I hearing things or is something coming toward this bedroom? It sounds like something lightly dragging on the carpet in the hallway. Oh God, they're coming, they're coming this way, they're coming for me! My minds' eye see's teeth bared in the fuzzy shapes approaching the door, four of them, no five of them, wait six; oh God how many are coming for me?

My heart pounds heavily as I press the bed tightly against the door and pull blankets over my head. **"GET AWAY FROM ME!"** I scream, my heart pounding furiously, **"WHO ARE YOU? GET AWAY, GET AWAY FROM ME!"** I feel like a child, but having the blankets over my head, and not being able to see them, is comforting.

After a few minutes of breathing stale air under the blankets, I realize it must not be the "boogey man", all is quiet. My mind must be playing tricks on me. What did I really see? My mind races as I try to recall what transpired just moments ago. Were there three of them, was it only two, could it have been four?

Wait! What was that? What did I just hear? OH GOD! It is a 'whoosh'! Someone, or something, flying past the door to this bedroom! A low moan, or growl, that increases and decreases in intensity as if they whirl about in a circle from this door, through the dining room to the kitchen where they begin and end.

Bracing myself against the wall, I press the bed against the door. The wall behind me cracks slightly from the pressure. Are they coming for me? My neck throbs as my heart pounds faster and faster. I press my feet harder against the bed.

THERE IT IS AGAIN! Louder this time, a throaty roar, increases and then decreases… Oh, wait! That sounded like… that sounded like a car! Is it only a car going by; or perhaps a pickup? Yeah, that's it! Phew! It is only a car passing the front of my house. I am freaking out! My feet drop to the floor. Ah shit! I try psyching myself up. "Come on you coward! There is nothing out there!"

I moved the bed and reached for the doorknob, but thought better of it. Perhaps I had not heard anything more dangerous than a car passing my window, but I did see something. Something was on the couch in my bedroom, there is no mistaking that. It was not clear, not distinct, but it had the shape of people! That door can remain closed for now!

I concentrate, desperately trying to recall the images I saw in my bedroom scant minutes ago. Yes... they were smallish people, maybe two to three feet tall, maybe four, but very thin people with sunken cheeks. The one that gave me a sinister look had a long pointy nose. Aw jeez, that sounds stupid, a long "pointy" nose. They were unclear, kind of fuzzy like, but not transparent - after all I did see them... didn't I? My mind races and heart pounds as I reach for the door knob to check my bedroom again. No, I can't go there yet. I strain to detect any sound coming from the direction of my bedroom... nothing. Holding my breath, I try to block out the sound of my heavy breathing and pounding heart... still nothing. Was it two men and a woman? I do not recall for certain.

Although early in the evening, I keep the bed pressed against the locked door, spread the blankets on the floor and reach for the light. My hand pulls back slowly from the switch. "Come on you coward, go ahead, turn the light off," I admonish myself; "You don't sleep with a light on." This night I do.

Chapter Two

Had it been Kay sitting on the edge of the couch in our bedroom, I would not have been surprised. I want to see her. I miss her so much. She passed away twenty-three days ago and the last of my guests for the funeral departed two weeks later. My brother Don stayed with me after Kay was cremated, but now I am alone. For almost the first time in my life, and the first time in eighteen years, I am alone.

God I miss her. She was sick for several years and had been getting worse. Others saw her steady decline, but I could not; or perhaps more accurately, would not. "She will get better," I kept saying.

We retired to my hometown in Minnesota two years ago, but a combination of cold winters and Kay missing her family, brought us back to Texas four months before she was hospitalized. The Doctors told me there was nothing to do but make her last days as pleasant as possible. There were only nine of those "last days".

I think about her almost constantly as I roam about our big house. The dog we acquired shortly after our wedding eighteen years ago; had to be put down just two weeks after Kay died. How she loved that little dog, hell I loved him too, and now I don't even have Puddles to keep me company.

I talk to Kay… yes, I talk to her, when no one is around I talk out loud, half expecting her to answer. Her ashes are with me and as I caress the brass urn tears well up in my eyes. I am not the crying sort so quickly shake it off, "Gotta be strong".

Busying myself with menial chores about the house, I had forgotten about my "guests" from last night. Late in the afternoon I walk into my bedroom and there they are. I stop, stare, wheel about, and dial 911 from my office.

"911 what's your emergency?" The dispatcher intones.

"There are intruders in my house." I respond.

"Are they there now sir?" she asks.

"Yes." I manage to answer, my voice barely above a whisper.

"What's the address sir? Officers will be there shortly; stay on the line with me."

It takes less than three minutes for the officers to arrive; apparently an intruder alert brings the cops in a hurry.

I meet the two patrol cars as they slide to a stop in front of the house. Two men jump out of the first car drawing guns from their holsters holding them away and toward the ground.

"Are they still in there?" the lead officer asks. I nod. A third officer from the second patrol car motions for me to come away from the house and takes my arm as we seek refuge behind his squad car. He is a very big man, perhaps six and a half feet tall with a powerful muscular frame. He makes my five foot ten inches and one hundred eighty pounds feel tiny. None of the officers wear hats and the big one pulling me behind the patrol car has short blond hair and reddish complexion. The other two, smaller in stature, but powerfully built, have their guns trained on my front door as they ease it open and shout a warning.

The big man questions me quietly about who is inside, keeping his eyes fixed on the house. He turns to look at me as I describe the tiny, nearly opaque figures. "I think they are two men and a woman, but I am not sure." I quickly spill out as much detail as I can.

It is only a couple of minutes before one of the officers comes from the house and asks, "Could they have gotten out the back door? It is unlocked."

I don't know how to respond and the larger and smaller officers exchange glances. All of a sudden, I feel foolish. It sounds stupid to me as well.

"They are ghosts." I say softly, almost apologetically. Thankfully neither of the officer's smile, or worse yet, burst into raucous laughter to ridicule me. They ask me what I saw, when they appear, what do they say, do I feel threatened, have they made any moves toward me, and many other questions I don't want to answer. They must think I am crazy, but there is no sign of patronization as I study their faces.

The youngest of the officers joins us and exclaims! "The house is clear." Continuing to question me, I detect a softening in their eyes when I mention Kay's passing. They probably think I am just some heartsick old man devastated by the loss of his wife. Well… I saw what I saw. Aw jeez! It is best not to pursue it any further.

"Do you want me to accompany you into the house?" the large officer asks. I hesitate, feeling like a small child being protected by a "grownup", I also wonder what good that would do, but acquiesce. "OK." I say softly.

I peer into the bedroom from the hall but see nothing. He asks gently. "Are they there?"

I laugh, "Of course not. They want me to look stupid to the police, obviously".

It is getting dark as I thank the officers, bid them farewell at the door, and return to the bedroom. There they are. Shit! I take a couple of steps toward the front door, but decide not to run after the police, and I surely will not call 911 again. The pounding in my chest, the quickening breath tells me the fear has returned.

Quickly I walk to the front door, grasp the doorknob, but do not turn it. If I leave the house, where will I go? Should I run? If I do, to where? Dawn lives about thirty miles away, should I go there? Removing my hand from the doorknob, I ponder my options.

I go cold, my ears are ringing; the hair standing up on the back of my neck. There is a presence, someone is approaching me from behind, and I whirl quickly, but there is no one in the hall. I know someone was there. Did I imagine it?

My office is to the right of the front door and I go to my desk and sit behind it. Staring at the floor, I occasionally lift my head and look at the street lights outside through the window, then toward my bedroom. My breath comes in short gasps from the fear and trembling. I can't go on like this, it must be resolved. Something must be done.

The desk chair rolls back as I stand up. Reluctantly I move away from this safe haven and make my way to the hallway. Standing in front of my bedroom, I look for something out of the ordinary, but then nothing is ordinary any more. Damn, my feet are heavy and do not want to move. I have been afraid before but this is different, am I in danger? I feel as if I am. Moving slowly toward my bedroom, I slide my feet along the floor as if maintaining contact will help me in case... in case what? In case I have to turn and run?

With a pounding heart, I ease into my bedroom. This time I will not run and hide. I stare at the... at the... at the what? They are small, very thin and seem to... to... shimmer? The images do not move as you think of moving, although they do turn their faces slightly toward me as I enter. They seem to ignore me, yet I feel they are aware of my presence. Appearing to be in one place, they suddenly move an inch or two one direction or the other, moving kind of herky jerky like, almost like... like, wait, like the figures in the movie Star Wars, what were they called? Holograms, I think. Yet they are not shimmering lights but semi-blurred, shimmering images of... of tiny people. When we die, do we become tiny ghosts? Is that what or who they are, ghosts?

"**Get out of here!**" I scream at them, my voice, hands and legs trembling with fear. They do not respond or acknowledge me. "What do you want?" I ask in a calmer tone, but my voice cracks and I am still trembling, do I really want to yell at them and make them mad? "Who are you?" I ask meekly, my mouth dry, voice cracking and just above a whisper.

They still do not acknowledge me although they heard me. What makes me think that, I do not know? One, then another looks at, or through me. Their eyes, there is something about their eyes. Wait! They have no pupils! Their eyes are… I look from one to another… blank. What color are they, the sinister looking large eyeballs, more black or dark gray than any other color and no pupils, or is it all pupils?

"Can you hear me?" I ask softly. There does not seem to be any imminent danger; they are not baring their teeth or growling at me. I feel fear and am prepared to run if necessary, although my legs are weak and arms hang limply at my side. Could I run? What if they suddenly lunge at me? Will I be able to lift my arms to defend myself or will I collapse in fear? They are not hideous beasts, just… tiny… almost people.

Something has to happen. Either I am crazy and seeing things, or these 'things' are real, I have to find out. Perhaps it is the angle with which I see them. Maybe if I move they will disappear. Slowly moving toward my bed, I keep as much distance as possible between us. Easing down on the edge of the bed, I turn my back to the couch and peer straight forward into the bathroom. For several moments I sit breathing heavily, wondering what to do next. Nothing has happened; I hear nothing, but my heavy breathing and pounding heart. My body tingles and my ears ring as I slowly turn and look over my left shoulder at them. They are ignoring me, but still there. I look away quickly, take a deep breath, and turn to face them and study them carefully. Their hands are relatively inactive yet moved, but didn't move; I'm not sure which. Two of them are female with features I do not recognize: straight hair the color of which is not discernible, (Blue?) sometimes darker, sometimes lighter, changing as I look from one to the other. The male has a rather long pointy nose, sunken cheeks, and blackish straight hair above his ears and a completely bald top. He looks more sinister than the women. Searching my memory, I cannot recall anyone that even vaguely fits his appearance. The clothing is almost like dirty rags, (old suits?) nearly indistinguishable, as the clothing is blurry but grayish in color.

"Sheesh!" I stand up and go into the bathroom closing the double doors behind me. When I come out a few minutes later they are gone. I lay in bed, looking over at the couch every few minutes, but they do not come back. Walking slowly toward the window, I draw back the curtain and look toward the sky for the position of the moon. Surely it must be a reflection... but how then could I see them in the daylight? I cannot see the moon. Other houses have lights in the windows but surely those dim lights could not cast a reflection that had the appearance of... humans? "Oh God. You idiot! Go to sleep."

"Kay." I call out softly from behind my desk as I sit up straight, the palms of my hands face down on my desk. It is just past noon and the sun no longer shines directly into my office windows facing east. No answer. "Kay?" I want her to answer. I desperately want her to answer, to show herself, to let me see her beautiful face again. She was voted the most beautiful girl in her senior class at Odessa Permian high school, retaining that beauty throughout her life. Some thought her illness diminished that beauty the last few years, but not me. "Can you hear me Kay?" I touch her urn, and speak softly to her. I need to talk to her. I need to talk to someone - Dawn!

"Hi dad!" Dawn answers the telephone jovially, as she always does when I call. "How are you getting along?" Her voice is soft, consoling as only a daughter can. It is less than a month since her step-mother passed away, God it's hard to say that... passed away.

Dawn is my daughter from my first marriage, and beautiful like her mother. She looks just like her mother except Dawn is blonde whereas Lila was a natural brunette. They both are tall, five foot seven with very trim figures. Perhaps I am biased, but Dawn is even more beautiful than her mother, who I always thought had Hollywood type looks. Dawn could stop traffic.

Dawn and I have been close for many years, ever since she graduated high school in Minnesota and came to live with me in Texas more than twenty years ago. Now, despite living only thirty miles apart, we do not see each other often, always too busy I rationalize. When we do talk, it is over the telephone; she has called me frequently since Kay's passing.

Today, as I pour out my tale to her, she listens quietly, politely interjecting questions. She comforts me by saying, "If I didn't know how level headed and rational you are dad, I would…" she didn't finish the statement. "If it were anyone else." she pauses for a few seconds. "But you see them, so they are there, end of story."

Suddenly, it feels as if a weight is lifted, a weight I had not been aware of, and I begin to relax. Just sharing what I see eases my mind.

"Will you call me if they come back dad?"

"Come back?" I say startled. "I'm looking at them right now." There is silence at the other end.

"They are there now?" She asks moments later with a sense of urgency in her voice.

"Yes."

"Dad. You need to get out of there right now." emphasizing 'now'. "Dad!"

"Dawn. You needn't worry. They appear to be harmless, or at least they've not threatened me." I don't mention the one that frightens me, no need to cause her undue concern.

"You're sure?"

"Yes, I can see them from the hallway outside my bedroom. They just sit there, calm as can be."

"Dad!" She pauses for several seconds as I wait for her to continue. "Dad, I have always been skeptical about ghosts, apparitions, and the like, but… wow, this is so new to me daddy. I'm not sure what to say." She pauses. "Do you want me to come over?"

"Nah." I laugh. "I'm OK. Really. I don't feel threatened; it's just… weird."

"Yeah. Weird." She laughs nervously. "Are you sure you're OK?" Before we finish our conversation, I know she has no reservations. I call my brother, Don.

"WOW! COOL! LITTLE GREEN MEN!" Don is excited about the possibility of actually encountering, at least through his brother, genuine UFO's. He believes that aliens are, or have been, here affecting our past as well as our present. He watches the sky in hopes of sighting something he expects to see.

"Don!" I laugh. "These are not little green men."

"How do you know?" He says, sounding hurt, and in truth I do not know. They look human-like, just very small. But then, what do 'little green men' look like?

We talked for some time about my 'guests', him excited about what he hopes they are and me... well, I am not exactly *excited* about them, although I don't think I fear them as much anymore. Apprehension is a better term although who knows, I do exercise caution around them and my blood does run a little cold.

The same ones do not come every day, as they appear somewhat different each time. Yesterday I believed there were two men and one woman. Strange, each time there are three of them, although possibly not the same three. Are they passing from one dimension to another? Have they recently died and are awaiting their final resting place? But why are there always three? Why not one, or two, or... or... nine?

Chapter Three

It is red brick isn't it? It must be as it is not grey or brown or black. It is not really red, or at least a very bright red. From my kitchen window I have a good view of my neighbor's house north of me. It is a beautiful house with an intriguing feature, a spiral staircase visible through the window halfway up a tower topped off by a conical roof.

I smile as I whisper a line from a childhood fairy tale, "Rapunzel, Rapunzel let down your hair". No one appears at the window.

The conical roof extends above the two story home and has a round brass ball at its peak. The driveway to their two car garage curves behind the 'tower' and I suspect if I would get up before eight in the morning I might see them depart for work. They return around six in the evening; I have heard them drive up. I don't recall seeing any children, but have not met them as we have not lived, wait...I have not lived here very long. God, it is hard not to include Kay in my thoughts and conversations. Yeah, they're probably at work I muse as I finish the last of my breakfast and last night's dinner dishes.

It is bright out, a nice sunny day. Whoops! There goes a shadow across the house next door, and I look up trying to see the cloud momentarily blocking the sun, but the angle is too great for me to see the sun to the southeast. Other fleecy clouds lazily move from west to east. I peer at the grass and the trees across the street for signs of a wind. Nope, but the clouds are moving so there must be a slight breeze at least.

My grandson Jeff should be here soon to mow my lawn.

It's ten-thirty AM as I open my third beer. Well, I have been up since nine, and I did have breakfast, if warmed-up pizza can be called breakfast, so... leave me alone. Holding a conversation with myself makes me laugh, 'gotta hold an intelligent conversation with someone' ha. Don't know why I ordered a medium pizza last night; didn't even get half of it finished. Better start ordering a small. Oh well, something to eat tonight and tomorrow.

I shouldn't drink a lot of beer I know, but... what else am I going to do? Earlier I drank my second beer on the patio eating my pizza breakfast and watching the golfers pass by.

It's nice living this close to a golf course, although I have not played much the past couple of years. Never a good golfer, my skill level has deteriorated, I don't recall the last time I broke a hundred. I do recall, proudly, the seventy-seven I carded several years ago, the first and only time I broke eighty, can't do that anymore.

My third beer half finished, I returned to the patio to watch and listen to the golfers. The green situated fifty yards behind my house is on a mound sloping from back to front away from me and I cannot see the surface of the green, or the golfers, from my house. I can however, discern by the coarse language and loud exclamation that someone just missed a putt. Chuckling to myself I wonder how many times have I done that, not swear, but miss an easy putt?

My best friend Dale would certainly enjoy this, as he is more of a golf-a-holic than I. He drove from Kansas City for Kay's funeral and stayed a couple days with me before returning home. Maybe I should call him and tell him about... ha... about what, my new friends? Will he think I am off my rocker? No, he won't; we have always been close, able to confide in one another about anything. He won't laugh at me now... will he?

Opening my fourth beer, I return to my patio chaise. The third one lasted almost an hour.

Somebody just missed a putt... whoa! Wash your mouth out with soap fella! There goes the putter flying through the air. Ha! Ha! Ha! At least I never got so upset that I threw a club, well, not like that anyway. That putter had to have gone twenty to thirty feet in the air. Wow! Here comes the golfer as a head bobs up over the rise of the green, then disappears as he bends to pick up the balky device. Continuing over the hill, he stops on the downward slope near the cart path, hands on his hips. Lightly holding the putter in the center of the shaft, he disgustedly looks to his right as his partners approach with the golf carts. His obscenity laced tirade apparently isn't a new reaction, for his partners say nothing as he slams the putter into his bag and sits down hard on the passenger side of the cart. Silently, they pull away to the next tee box. Looks like a 'fun' day for three of them, I muse. They probably will have a hearty laugh at the miffed man but, I suspect not in his presence.

Dale and I just laugh at each other when we mess up on the course, and we get plenty of laughs, ha. He loves throwing digs at me such as; "You're gonna love that one" as my ball sails deeply into the woods, or; "Tough lie, how long can you tread water?" as my ball settles in a pond.

It truly is a beautiful day as I watch the few fleecy white clouds slowly drift by. With only a whisper of a breeze, the shadow of a cloud passing over noticeably cools the temperature, which is in the lower eighties, not bad for an October day. Leaning back in the chaise, I soak up the sun warming my face.

Was I dozing? The sky is nearly white as I open my eyes. Blue colors return to the sky as my eyes adjust and I watch the clouds lazily pass. The shapes of the clouds slowly change as I recall a game played as a child, trying to name various items or shapes in the clouds. That one doesn't have much shape, just an elongated ball much longer than it is tall. Hmm. It does remind me of... a brain. Yeah, with folds throughout the top, front and back, it looks like pictures I have seen of a brain. Not as dark though. This 'brain' could not be called grey matter as it is almost totally white. The brain even has a short stem coming down from the back and the various folds. Hmmm, what are the functions of those folds? What area controls what? Watching the figure of the brain, I am dismayed as it seems to be dissipating. The figure shrinks slowly to barely a wisp of a cloud. Clouds must go away with age.

A mower starts up; Jeff is here, so I gulp down the remainder of my beer. Oh shoot! I need to take the garbage out to the curb as the truck comes mid afternoon.

Opening the garage door, I wave to Jeff as he makes his rounds in front of the house.

"How ya doin' grandpa!" he yells over the roar of the small engine and goes about his business. He mows several lawns each day, which he has done for three years now, and at nineteen seems content to make this his life's work, not that he has to worry about work. His great grandfather on his Dad's side made sure of that in the oil fields many years ago and now Jeff, his dad, and my daughter only work at what they enjoy and not to earn a living, must be nice. Jeff has grown his business nicely as he does make a pretty good income from it.

I can't complain, having retired two years ago as vice-president of sales for a fortune 500 company, I am enjoying a handsome pension. It is fortunate I retired when I did as I was able to spend more time with Kay before she… before she…

My garbage can is a plastic bin on wheels provided by the city of Plano, and rarely filled to the halfway point, and then mostly with beer cans. I really shouldn't drink as much as I do but…

"Hello." I yell to my neighbor across the street as he too is rolling his garbage out to the curb. "Rick Hageman," I say as I walk across the street extending a hand to my neighbor. This is the first time I have seen him and decide it will be nice to get to know my neighbors.

He is probably in his forties, at least twenty years my junior, and very neatly dressed with black slacks and a pastel blue long sleeved dress shirt buttoned to the top and at the wrists. The collars and cuffs are moderately starched. It is my nature to dress neatly, but today with a casual grey polo above tan slacks, I am very much out-dressed. He is a thin man a little over six feet in height with short crew cut brown hair, a hairstyle straight from the fifties. With my slicked back thinning grey hair, I am somewhat envious of his thicker stand of hair, even if it is a throwback style. We are approximately the same weight, even though he must be three inches taller and I am not fat, well I could stand to lose a few pounds. No, at one hundred eighty I probably outweigh him by ten to twenty pounds. His skin is very even in color and texture...wait, is he wearing makeup? Surely not, he must have a pasty complexion. I try not to stare as I study his face.

"Lance Burkhart," he replies tentatively as he lightly takes my hand and steps back slightly. I unintentionally squeeze his hand too hard.

"I suppose you saw the party going on last night." I open, feeling it necessary to at least try to explain the police visit last night.

"Oh no! Bruce and I did not party last night, no, no, we were home all night by ourselves, no visitors, no party." he replies nervously backing away.

I am taken aback by this response and as I formulate my explanation as to the meaning of 'party' it is obvious he misunderstands, thinking I was talking about him having a party. I suspect he values his privacy and that of... of... did he say Bruce? Uh Oh! Now I get it, the stereotype names, the pasty complexion, the light handshake, the thin stature and the... OK, I admit it. I am homophobic I guess, and wow, am I standing in the middle of the street talking to... one of them, and he lives across the street?

Jeff is loading his mower before I finish talking with... did he say Lance? Excusing myself as painlessly as possible, I return to the safety of my own home.

The chimney, of a yet to be used fireplace, peeks over the crest of my roof and is framed by meandering white fleecy clouds. I marvel at how their shape subtly fluctuates, rolling as one side rises and the other falls, billows of cottony fleece alternately separating and folding together. I'll think of the shapes later on my patio. The crest of the roof makes a ninety degree turn culminating in a triangle at the east end of the garage. Kay loved this house; it's my house alone now.

Jeff has loaded his mower onto the small trailer he pulls behind a ten year old Ford pickup. His story is similar to many whose grandfathers' or great grandfathers' hit it big in the oil fields during the early 1900's. However; to his credit and that of his family, they are not affected by great wealth. Jeff, as his parents, works industriously at tasks that allow him to "earn his own way". By their attitude and attire they are not presumptuous but are what people of my upbringing admire and call, "just regular folks".

Dad was a painter that walked stooped over, a result of a bout with Polio shortly after my birth. Although unable to stand upright without bending his knees and placing a hand to his back, he and Uncle Lyle were out early to brighten the exteriors or interiors of other people's homes. Mother was a seamstress and sales lady for a woman's apparel store downtown. Together they provided a modest home and living for their two sons and two daughters.

As I enter the shaded entryway to my house and grasp the large brass door handle, the air is noticeably cooler than that across the street. Opening the door, the air conditioned cool air from the inside wafts gently over me as I step in. Pausing momentarily, I glance to my right at the "Office", a room that has not served that function for business since my retirement over two years ago. I look down the twelve foot long corridor leading to the master guest bedroom that was my sanctuary last night. A cold chill engulfs me as I recall last night's events. Brrr.

Directly across from the office is a shorter hallway leading to a third bedroom straight ahead. To the right in the hallway is the third bathroom, the second being in the master guest bedroom. Opposite the third bathroom is a nook containing the washer and dryer before extending to the interior door to the garage. Behind the wall of the laundry, and also across from the third bathroom, is the fourth bedroom filled with boxes, yet to be unpacked, and items from our return from Minnesota.

Further down the hall ahead is the master bedroom and bathroom where last night... well, I prefer to look to my right as I pass the formal dining room and enter the living room.

I glance briefly above the double bay windows at the small window replaced after being struck by an errant golf ball. It is baffling how a window ten feet in the air can be struck from a distance of fifty to sixty yards behind the tenth green. Was it a shot accidently over-clubbed from a short distance, or was it intentional? At any rate, I am glad it did not strike one of the more expensive bay windows.

During inclement weather, I sit sipping coffee and reading the newspaper in my kitchen. On good days, which are most days, I exit through the door on the west side of the kitchen to the patio. There I sit and watch the receding shade from the rising sun and listen to the sounds of wind, birds and golfers.

On the patio again with beer number five, I am amazed I can drink that much beer in so short a time span and not feel a buzz. I always have been able to hold my liquor. My fifth beer, and I have been up just under five hours, not bad, a little behind my usual pace. I'll probably do my average of a twelve pack again today, can't do much more as I would have to go to the store to get more and don't feel like going out today.

I sweep grass clippings off my stone patio. It takes Jeff almost more time to unload and load his mower than to mow my small yard. He does it because I am his grandfather and to help me out. I pay him of course, but for the time he spends here he could make more money at a larger yard, but then again, money isn't everything to him. He is a good boy, works very hard.

OK! It is five O'clock and I have had what, eight, nine, ten beers? I don't know. Why should I care how many; they don't really affect me, although I do feel a slight buzz. I should eat something, but I'm not hungry. Pizza! I'll have more of last night's pizza. Shall I eat it cold or warm it up like I did for breakfast? Ah the hell with it, I'll just eat it out of the cardboard box and have another beer.

Taking a bite out of the second piece of cold pizza, I notice the clouds have darkened considerably from earlier in the day. The wind also picked up and the temperature has dropped, although surely still in the seventies. There is a cold wisp of air and a sudden fresh, sweet smell. It's going to rain soon. The dark clouds move much faster than the white billowy clouds from this morning and seem closer to the ground, although the clouds higher above do not appear to be moving at all. A storm could be brewing as there are much darker, almost purple, clouds on the western horizon. Walking around to the front to bring in my garbage container, the sky is still very light and blue toward the east, not like that on the other side of the house.

Closing the lid on the pizza, I feel a cool breeze for a moment and smell the fresh scent detected minutes ago. I suddenly harbor a thought that perhaps it is not the fresh scent that precedes a rain, what if it is... *them* coming back.

Ah shit! I hadn't thought about them today, but now... how can I think of anything else? Are ghosts or apparitions, or whatever, accompanied by a cool breeze and the slight scent of freshness? It can't be, after all I had recognized the smell of freshness and the cool breeze many times prior to a rain. Normally the breeze and freshness preceded the rain by less than an hour and... Oh God! Could it always have been... ghosts seeking shelter from an approaching storm? Could they have passed by me, or through me, on their way toward a safe haven? Could the sweet freshness I smelled have been their perfume or body scent? I cannot say body odor as it's always a pleasant odor, I mean scent... damn!

The sky is darkening quickly now and the wind has picked up dramatically. A couple of golfers appear on the berm around 'my' green and peer skyward. They speak to one another speculating on how much longer they can play. "You won't finish the back nine," I voice softly, "as this is the tenth hole and the storm will be here before you can finish. Better hurry!" The wind blows the pizza box toward the edge of the patio table and I catch it before it falls. Gotta save tomorrow's breakfast I laugh.

I try not to think about the 'people' that may be in my bedroom as I put the pizza back in the refrigerator; I don't look in that direction. I am not ready to confront that again just yet. Opening another beer, I turn on the television in the family room.

I cannot help but cast furtive glances toward my bedroom and strain my ears to listen over the drone of the television to hear any sounds coming from that room. The program on television cannot keep my attention, although I try for several minutes to listen. My attention is drawn toward the bedroom.

My heart nearly stops as I hear a slow moan that dies away as quickly as it came. What was that? The house is shaking slightly. My dry mouth is open, blood cold as if drained from my body, heart pounding, and stomach fluttering nervously. This is fear! Yes, this is a much greater fear than the first time I saw them. They must be angry! Are they in there? Wait, there it is again, only louder, the moaning, and, it's...it's coming from behind me! Oh, you God damned coward! That is only the wind vibrating downspouts or a portion of the house that is loose.

From the kitchen window I watch the start of a heavy downpour, hearing the wind as it blows on the eaves and downspouts creating a harmonic low guttural howling sound that starts and stops in no particular pattern. The rain begins with a few large drops that make a great splashing noise a few seconds apart as they contact the house, the patio furniture and the ground. In the dim light of late afternoon, I see large dark splotches as the rain strikes the concrete patio and splashes on the glass table top outside.

The initial splashes and loud plops of the large raindrops grow to a crescendo as the rain greatly intensifies and the wind blows it nearly horizontal with the ground. WOW! This is the beginning of **some** storm. Water puddles on the patio and furniture. The heavy rain coming down almost horizontally in silver white sheets obliterates my view of the golf course. The volume of noise from rain striking the house oscillates up and down as the rain intensifies and decreases rapidly. The slope of the berm at the back of the tenth green is barely discernible now.

The television program holds no interest so I do not turn up the volume to hear the dialogue over the pounding rain and howling of the wind. Time for another beer I rationalize, and go to the kitchen window to peer out again at the storm. Lightning flashes and the clap of thunder follows a scant six seconds later. What is the formula for distance of a lightning strike, five seconds per mile? I think that is right. The back door vibrates slightly back and forth from the wind, which is surprising as I thought the door was tight. No water comes through as I check the kitchen floor in front of the door.

Another brilliant flash and I count, "One thousand one, one thousand two, one thou..." BOOM! Wow! That was a loud one, and getting closer too! It is quite dark out now although there is at least an hour before sunset; the only light is that provided by the television and lightning storm, and what an impressive storm.

I see flashes of light from my bedroom hallway simultaneously with the light flashing through the family room windows. I know it is only the lightning, but I did not anticipate the lightning flashes to be so readily seen through the heavy drapes on the bedroom windows, or is it... oh damn! Could it be... them? Are the draperies open, or are 'they' creating the light? My ears are ringing and I feel fear, or at least apprehension. With each lightning flash, shapes and patterns form on the walls, the ceiling, and the floor. How can the shapes change from one flash to another? It should always be the same

41

shape, right? Is someone or something manipulating the light?

THERE… IT IS HIM! The pointy nosed guy comes out of my bedroom, looks at me as he glides across the hall into my dining room. He is behind the wall, I can't see him. OH GOD! What is he going to do? Is he… will he…?

Grasping a throw pillow from the couch, I pull my knees up and clutch the pillow to my face, tightly closing my eyes at every lightning flash and flinching at the subsequent crash of thunder, now occurring almost simultaneously. Is he coming for me? Should I go somewhere? Where can I go? HE'S GOING TO GET ME!

The wind rages harder and the vibrations shake the house as if it is about to be blown down. "Little pig, little pig." I try to laugh, recalling the story of the big bad wolf. The pillow is of little comfort but at least I cannot see if he is coming. Pulling the throw pillows on the couch over me to hide, I fear, is he going to grab me? I don't want to know and I should run, but to where? There is no other sound but the howling wind, pounding rain and creaking of the house.

Finally the lightning flashes and thunder grow farther apart and the wind slowly begins to subside. Perhaps I can relax now and see if the 'pointy nosed one' is still there. Am I alone? I tentatively pull the pillow down and scan the room, seeing no one. Biting on the pillow's fringe, I decide not to seek him out. If he is here… well, I don't want to know. Once again I bury my face in a throw pillow.

Television still does not interest me but I must have dozed off, for my beer is lukewarm. Oh well, there is only a quarter of a can left anyway. The storm has subsided considerably but it is still dark outside. I look at the clock in amazement, it is almost nine o'clock! I slept for almost two hours!

Opening the refrigerator, I am surprised to find there are only two beers left. When the day started I had a twelve pack plus about half of a twelve pack. The half pack was finished much earlier I realize, but surely I did not drink sixteen or seventeen beers today. Subconsciously, I turn to my right and although my bedroom is not visible from this position in the house, I look toward that room. Can they… do they… did they have some of my beer? Is that what the 'pointy nosed one' was after, my beer?

I pull the next to last can out of the refrigerator and lean lightly on the door. No, if he can pass through walls, he surely cannot pick up an object such as a beer can besides, I would have heard the refrigerator door open… you stupid shit; he can pass right through the door, he doesn't need to open it. Wait a minute. He can't make the cans of beer pass through the door can he? He has to open the door to get the can of… oh damn, get real Rick. My brain is becoming frazzled from too much thought; I need to go to bed. Whoa! Not yet, I am not ready to enter that room again just yet. But maybe tonight they are not in there; maybe I was just imagining things and didn't really see them.

I close the refrigerator door and after opening the can, take two great pulls from it emptying more than half its contents. With apprehension, I slosh the contents lightly back and forth and back up in the kitchen to where the hallway to my bedroom can be seen. A three foot entryway leads into my bedroom with the door normally open. No light comes from the room, and why should there be, the lights are off during the day, no reason to burn them needlessly. Straining my eyes, I expect to see some sort of light caused by... them. I want to go to bed but can't get my feet to move from the kitchen floor. I must know; is the 'pointy nosed one' waiting for me? Are they there? With heavy feet, I finally detach one foot then the other from the floor and creep slowly toward my bedroom. "Oh God, please don't let them be there."
They are.

Chapter Four

She has such a pretty face. I accept the hand extended in greeting, and smile recalling what was said whenever we saw a fat girl and didn't want to be mean, "Oh she has such a pretty face." It means of course, "she would be OK if she would lose that balloon body." Fat girls are rarely popular, almost shunned, more so than fat boys, which somehow never quite seemed improper. Girls are supposed to be thin, prim and proper while boys can be, well, whatever.

"What can I do for you this morning sir?" She has a sweet sounding voice and, to be fair, she really is not all that fat just... big boned. With a chuckle, I remember another descriptive term. Big boned... give me a break! It means she has to cover those big bones with more meat. She is overweight, but in today's society it is improper to consider that as being fat. Oh no, cannot say what we mean, must be politically correct!

"Hi. My name is Rick Hageman." Smiling as I introduce myself, keeping secret thoughts to myself. And she does have a pretty face, reddened cheeks puff up a bit too much... there I go again, just focus on her as the bank officer you have to deal with and leave it at that.

I continue. "My wife just passed away and I have come to transfer the funds from her savings accounts and CD's over to my name."

"Your wife just passed away? I'm sorry to hear that Mr...."

"Hageman."

"I'm so sorry sir."

"Thank you, I appreciate that."

"And what was your wife's name Mr. Hageman?" She began stroking the keys of her computer, focusing on the screen.

"Kay."

She deftly enters information on her computer as she queries me about account numbers, social security numbers, birth dates, and the like. She peers intently at the screen, smiles at me, and excuses herself. "One moment Mr. Hageman, I'll be right back." She smiles sweetly as she strides past me.

I casually note how her neat blue dress does not cover the bulging hips, waist or oversized arms. An H shaped one inch wide white trim around her bodice appears stretched. The bulges around her hips bounce as she walks and I note the depressions created in the area of her bra straps and panty lines. Would a fashion guru recommend she wear a more loosely fitting dress? Well, this dress is not just tight but revealed evidence of... overweightedness. I love coining new words and smile at the humor created.

The bank is a simple satellite branch with four glass enclosed teller stations facing two desks for bank officers, one of which is the Brenda waiting on me, and another younger prettier officer. Why didn't I wait for her? Because, silly, the pretty one was already with a customer and you got stuck with, 'Oh she has such a pretty face'. Behind the tellers is the working area where they also handle drive up customers.

"Mr. Hageman?" The deep voice startles me as I turn sharply toward an older gentleman, well, probably not even my age. He smiles pleasantly at me and extends his hand. This is the stereotypical bank manager, tall, slim, thick grey hair, a man exuding an aura of wealth.

"Yes." I rise from my chair and take his hand.

"Would you mind coming with me?" He asks. Brenda stands behind him and flashes a quick smile as she looks away. I cast a puzzled glance at them as he motions toward a glass enclosed office.

"Take a seat sir." He pleasantly indicates a plush leather arm chair as he closes the door. Stepping around to sit in his chair, he rolls it up to the desk, quickly shuffles some papers together in a neat pile and sets them aside. "Now Mr. Hageman, I understand you wish to transfer some funds from your wife's account into yours, is that correct?"

"Yes." That irritates me, I told fatso that several minutes ago. Calm down Rick, be patient, it is probably standard procedure for a higher ranking bank official to handle a transaction of this size. After all, the two hundred dollars a month I put into various accounts for Kay the past fifteen years has grown to over ninety-seven thousand dollars. This is money we planned on using to take Kay's daughter from her first marriage, along with the son-in-law, for an extended tour of the U.S. or parts of Europe. Chase and I get along OK, but Angel never liked or respected me. She was sixteen when her mother and I married and early on I sensed a distance between us.

"And your wife is deceased?" The bank Vice President continues.

"Yes, a little over a month ago." I am repeating myself.

"Do you... ah... happen to have a probate judgment declaring you beneficiary of your wife's accounts?"

Judgment? I am taken aback by that term. Why would I need a judgment? What is mine is hers and what's hers is mine, isn't that the premise of marriage? "I'm not sure I understand, what do you mean by probate judgment? It is a joint account, hers and mine."

"Well no sir Mr. Hageman, it is not a joint account but in your wife's name only." He starts, with a little bounce in his chair. Now he sounds condescending and I don't like this man anymore. "When one passes away with substantial assets," he continues, smug in his 'I'm smarter than you' attitude, "One normally leaves a Will detailing how those assets are to be distributed. Do you have such a document?"

"Yes of course I do." I respond, unable to mask my irritation. We drew up our Wills over five years ago as we prepared for my retirement, but I had not given any thought to them for some time. My Will left almost everything to Kay and hers to me with a smaller portion being given to our natural daughters. My 401K and separate stock portfolios are close to a million dollars which, with my company pension and social security, will keep us in a decent quality of lifestyle throughout retirement.

"Then it should be a simple matter of having the probate judge issue the proper orders to release her assets to you or to the beneficiary." He stands up. "Bring that order to me, and I will gladly handle that transaction for you Mr. Hageman."

"You mean I cannot transfer my money from my wife's account into mine?"

"I'm sorry sir, not without a probate order."

"But it is my money!" My irritation is getting the best of me. "I can access my account any time I want to!"

He no longer has that smug look on his face. He did not anticipate me arguing so strenuously with him. "Yes sir, you can access your account but this is her account, it is not a joint account, and it is the law, I'm sorry but there is nothing I can do about it."

"That's bullshit!"

"Now sir, please." That is a condescending tone.

It is obvious this meeting is over. I refuse to shake the hand he extends and briskly leave his office and nod toward the big boned fat girl smiling briefly at me as she attends to a customer seated at her desk. This did not go as anticipated.

I call my friend Dave, a lawyer in San Antonio, who assisted us in drawing up our wills six years ago.

"It's easy. Just bring her Will to a probate lawyer, I will identify one for you, and he'll take care of everything for you. You have nothing to worry about." He says reassuringly.

"But Dave..., Kay did not sign her Will. Does that make a difference?" There is silence on the other end of the telephone.

"She didn't."

"No."

Dave sighs. "That probably throws a monkey wrench into the situation, but I don't know for sure. I'm not well versed on probate law. I suspect the law will look at her not signing the Will as an indication she did not agree with its contents and disregard it altogether."

"But she just never got around to signing it Dave; you know what her intentions were."

"I know Rick, but it doesn't matter what I know, or you know, about her intentions. What matters is what is written in a legal document properly filed with the courts and, from what you are telling me, I gather neither of you got around to filing your wills with the courts, is that a fair assumption?"

"Dave, mine is signed and notarized, but Kay... well... she just never got around to doing it. Perhaps I should have been more diligent in making sure she did, but... well, you know."

"Yes, I know." Dave sighs. After a pause he continues, "Let me contact a probate lawyer in your area, one with good credentials, and have him contact you. But Rick, I think in Texas your spouse is entitled to half your assets if not designated otherwise but... I think Angel will be entitled to a large portion of Kay's half, but let's wait to hear from the experts."

"Half of my assets?" I exclaim.

"Let's not get excited yet, let's wait to hear from the probate system." Dave is not reassuring.

"Dave. Kay did not work. All her assets were purchased by my earnings; she did not contribute to any of the accounts. She had no earnings."

"I know, I know, but that makes no difference in the eyes of the law, assets are distributed equitably among the heirs unless stated differently."

"So I'll get to keep some of what I put in?"

"Presumably."

The office building of Wilbur, Sheats and Howard is a lavish building that screams of opulence. The firm occupies the upper three floors of the twelve story glass building. My contact, Thomas Howard, is a partner in the firm and Dave warned me he would be expensive but is the top rated probate attorney in upper Texas. Reaching for something to read, I wait in the plush lobby that reminds me of a basketball court in size, only with granite floors and extremely high arched ceilings. Opaque glass windows on each end of the 'basketball court' provide light but not direct sunlight to the area. Many desks line the circumference of this level fifty or so feet away from where I sit. Several secretaries occupy the desks as well as some young men carefully dressed in business suits. Muffled laughter comes from a cubicle behind the exposed desks as a young man returns to his desk.

Large spiral staircases rise from each side in the middle of the lobby to the second floor balcony overlooking the lobby. A third floor balcony overhanging the second floor must be accessible only by elevator as there is no apparent staircase, and also much less activity on that floor. Executive suites I opine, very posh.

In the center of the 'basketball court' the reception desk is manned by two young receptionists that are very pleasant as well as extremely beautiful. I try to occupy my time reading a magazine in the waiting area 'Barbara' directed me to, but do not have much interest in Forbes or Money magazines. Although not disinterested in financial matters, I let my broker and tax adviser worry about that. Hmmm, no Sports Illustrated, guess I'll make believe I am reading the latest on Bill Gates.

It is twenty minutes past my appointment time when Barbara rises from her desk and begins to walk toward me, a bright smile bracing her lips. She is a tall girl, near six feet, a tight black skirt the hem of which is about halfway between her hips and her knees. A gold pull over top glistens as if metallic, tightly stretches where it ought to be stretched accentuating a narrow waist. There is an intriguing bounce to the front of her blouse as she clicks her way across the granite floor on five inch heels. The top of that blouse is adorned by what appears to be folds of a scarf the same color as the blouse but upon closer inspection, I try not to stare, it is part of the blouse. The 'scarf' starts from her shoulder and expands slightly as it crosses her bust line, finishing over the opposite shoulder. Shiny black hair cascades over her shoulders and a gold chain adorns her throat. Damn! They hire movie starlets for receptionists. Thirty years ago, no, not even twenty years ago, I may have had some lustful feelings but now… I just admire her beauty.

"Would you follow me Mr. Hageman?" She asks politely, and I rise without comment and fall in beside her as we walk to a cubicle near one end of the 'basketball court.' We engage in mundane small talk about the beautiful weather as we walk, finally stopping in front of the desk. With a bright smile, she says, "Mr. Lambert will see you now, sir."

"Mr. Lambert? I have an appointment with Mr. Howard." I say confused.

"Yes sir," she smiles demurely, "but Mr. Lambert will meet with you first." She peers directly into my eyes as she gestures for me to enter the cubicle.

"Mr. Hageman!" A young man in his late twenties or early thirties exclaims getting up from his desk. "Thank you Barbara, and Barbara. Did Mr. Hageman have some coffee?"

"Can I get you anything Mr. Hageman?" Barbara asks politely. It sounds rehearsed.

"No thank you, I'm fine." Turning to the young man, I do not mask my concern, "I thought I was to meet with Mr. Howard?"

"Yes sir and you will, but I am to handle the preliminary investigations and present my findings, which Mr. Howard will review and consult with you at a later time." Once he feels I am satisfied with his explanation, he continues to lay out some of the preliminary points for discussion.

Satisfied is not one of the thoughts that came to mind as my business is being shuttled off to an underling. Underling, I am amused as I imagine the 'overlings' having a much more opulent office than this. His cubicle externally resembles the others in that they appear to be ten to twelve feet square. One wall is occupied with a twelve foot high floor to ceiling bookcase almost completely filled with official looking books. His desk is Cherry wood neatly polished to a bright smooth finish, a computer on the left corner and a manila envelope boldly printed with my name, in the center of the desk.

A number jolts me back to what he is saying. "Excuse me, what did you say... how much did you say?"

"Why... five hundred per hour, but we anticipate it should not take more than twenty or so hours to bring your case to a resolution." he replies, looking puzzled at my question. I must appear stunned as he began to speak again. "Of course it could take less time but that is hard to say right now, it depends on the complexity of the issues. It may take longer."

No wonder they have such an opulent office building, ten thousand dollars for a few hours work, ridiculous! I feel heat rising in my temples and ringing in my ears as I quickly glance from side to side. "Am I being charged for our meeting now?"

"Why... ah, no sir. This meeting is to explain the process and enter into an agreement..."

"Then I will be on my way, thank you. No need to call Barbara, I can find my way out."

54

Attorneys are queried about hourly rates and estimated time to resolve on the telephone before agreeing to an appointment. After calling five or six attorneys listed in the yellow pages, I call Dave to ask him about the one that offers the lowest cost per hour.

"Rick, do you want the cheapest or the best?" Dave asks. "The best is Thomas Howard, but he is expensive. Do not hire the cheapest lawyer. Give me the names and let me get back to you."

Dave calls the next afternoon; "The cheap guy has a good reputation although relatively inexperienced, having been a probate attorney for under three years. I believe he will do a good job for you."

I find Monty Sterns' office in a strip mall off the tollway and obviously he is not supporting an opulent office. He must have hired his mother as a receptionist as she certainly does not compete with 'Barbara' for looks. She is as old as I am and smiles brightly when I announce myself. Checking her appointment book and leaning to her right, she says in a voice louder than normal conversation, "Mr. Hageman is here Monty."

"Thank you." came the reply from the office to her right. The office window overlooking the, ahem, reception area, is covered by pictures, calendars, boxes and other papers taped to the glass. Ah, very informal, I think I like this already.

"You may go right in sir." There is no door, only an opening in the wall where she indicated and I peer around the corner at a young man seated at a messy desk. His office is not much more than ten feet square. He has reference books stacked on the floor on top of one another along the wall.

"Come on in." He says not getting up, and points to a straight back chair with a well-worn seat. He is young, early to mid thirties with a square set jaw and powerful build. Looks like a linebacker. "You have some issues with a Will?" Gets right to the point doesn't he? I hand him the Will and take a seat.

He quickly reads the document, peering at the back of each page, then flips through all three pages, sets it down and looks at me. "It is a pretty standard Will, why didn't your wife sign it?"

"I thought she had, I may have been out of town shortly after we had them drawn up. She must have forgotten to sign hers in front of a notary. I never thought about it not being done when I returned."

He has his hand on his chin as he studies me. Finally he leans forward and asks, "Is it possible she had misgivings about the Will?"

"No! None whatsoever! We discussed our desires for quite some time before having the Wills drawn up. There was never a doubt as to our intent, either of us! I can't... I mean she... well she was somewhat forgetful sometimes, I mean she had been sick for a long time... she would forget things." I was uneasy and rambling.

He waited for me to slow down and start breathing steadily before he gently asked, "What was the nature of her illness?"

The fluorescent light began to blink in the outer room and the receptionist hollers, "Monty, this damn light is blinking again!"

"I'll stop and get some bulbs tonight, Mom." He yells in return. She is his mother. "I apologize for the interruption." He smiles nodding toward the outer room before continuing, "The nature of her illness?"

"Well, she had problems with her feet. The doctor called it Peripheral Neuropathy and she had great pain and difficulty walking the past five years."

"There was nothing they could do for her?" He seems genuinely interested and I began to feel more at ease with him.

"They gave her medication but..." I pause, wringing my hands together. This conversation seems to be heading in a direction I do not want to go, yet feel inevitably drawn to go there. "They ah,... they told her she could get better if she would ah,... if she would ah..."

"If she would stop drinking?" He interrupts.

My head jerks up angrily.

"I'm sorry; I had an aunt with Peripheral Neuropathy the family attributed to alc... excessive drinking. I say that, in spite of Doctors' telling us there is no connection between alcohol and the disease, but I believe it had something to do with it. My aunt was in great pain and also died far too young."

I nod, my anger subsiding.

"OK." He leans back in his creaking chair and swivels to his left. Resting his elbows on the wooden arms of the chair, his chin supported on his fingertips.

"She was forgetful." He slowly states. For several minutes he is in thought, then suddenly sits upright saying; "OK, let me see what I can do. I will call you tomorrow, or the day after for sure. In the meantime keep your chin up, although I don't want to give you false hope. This may be an uphill battle but, we'll see."

"Mr. Hageman, this is Monty Sterns." He states after I answer the telephone. "You didn't tell me your step-daughter, and her husband, are lawyers."

"Why is that important?" I answer perplexed.

"The only importance is… well they filed attachments on your wife's assets and joint assets. Do I have your permission to contact your step-daughter?"

"What do you mean they filed attachments?" I am not as angry as I may sound, just puzzled by what he means.

"It means she is claiming half of your assets, your wife's half, as her surviving next of kin, and in all probability, will be legally entitled to that judgment."

"Whoa!" His words sting, "Now… now… wait just a minute!" I stammer. "None of Kay's assets were earned by her, I was the breadwinner, the sole earner in the family; she did not work ever since we were married. All her accounts were contributed to by me, no one else, why is that not my money?"

Monty does not respond immediately. Finally he responds apologetically; "In the state of Texas Mr. Hageman, the couple shares assets jointly and without a written order, a Will, to the contrary, her portion of the assets go to her next of kin, in this case you and her daughter."

"I am her husband, her next of kin!" I sound exasperated even to myself.

"Yes sir, but in the eyes of the law, so is her daughter."

Chapter Five

"Can he be here already?" I see the headlights of a car bouncing into the driveway. It's only eleven-thirty. He said he wouldn't be here until after midnight and probably closer to one A.M.. Dale has a long drive from Kansas City and had to work until after three in the afternoon, surely he can't be here this soon?

"Hey!" I exclaim opening the door to see my best friend getting out of his van.

"Hey yourself, you old som-bitch!" He retorts.

"Whadda ya mean, you're older'n me!" I shoot back and we share a laugh and a hug as we greet one another. It hasn't been that long since we saw each other, at Kay's funeral in August, but it is always good to see someone you consider a brother and not just a childhood friend. He is six months older, and at six feet four inches and two hundred thirty pounds, much bigger than I. He is in great shape for a big man sixty-four years old and we constantly tease one another about who has the most hair, although neither of us can lay claim to having much.

"Are they here?" Dale asks, his smile waning. "Are your 'buddies' here tonight..., here now?"

I nod; I confided in him via telephone just four days ago and he immediately said he would arrange his work schedule so he could come see me. I told him he didn't have to, but he adamantly declared he did. Besides, he told me with a laugh, "It will give me an opportunity to kick your ass in golf again."

Much of the tension drains out of my body as he moves toward the front door. Now I will be vindicated, someone will lend credibility to my 'visitors' actually being here. Someone else will see them for what they are. I lead him into my bedroom and point at them sitting on my couch. He stares for a few seconds without expression, his eyes darting from side to side.

He finally says apologetically; "Rick, I don't see them. I'm sorry... I want to... but I don't."

I see the disappointment in his eyes and turn toward my 'guests', but... they are gone! This is a shock, as they were sitting on the couch when we entered the room. Stepping toward the couch, I move some of the throw pillows; but they are not under them. My bed; did I catch a glimpse of one of them slipping under my pillow? I pick up the pillow... damn, not there!

"Rick." Dale starts softly, "I guess I shouldn't be surprised I can't see them. They are real to you, but not to anyone else. I know you see them but... for whatever reason, you see them but I cannot."

I was certain he would be able to see them as we are so close that he feels what I feel and vice versa. They were there. Why will they not show themselves to Dale? Where did they go? The dirty sons-a-bitches.

"How 'bout a beer after my long drive?" Dale asks breaking the silence and bringing us back to the present.

"Yeah, sure." I nod, my eyes fixed on the spot where my 'buddies' normally reside. "You got here a lot earlier than I expected. I thought you said it was a ten hour drive." I head for the refrigerator.

"Normally it is, but I only stopped once on the way down whereas normally I stop at least twice, stretch my legs and take a nap for twenty to thirty minutes. The only time I did stop was for gas and to get a quick bite to eat on the way. I never did get sleepy, anxious to get here I guess." He takes a long pull from his bottle of beer. He prefers the glass bottles over the cans, while I still drink from the can. I smile as I recall why he said he couldn't drink from a can anymore; 'Seems like after thirty to forty cans I really get sick.' Duh, of course. It's his joke as he does not drink very much.

"So, tell me more about the little bastards." He began after setting the bottle down, nearly three-fourths of its contents gone. I describe as much detail as I recall about what I see and when, how I feel and what they do. We talk for nearly an hour and he is almost done with his second beer when he says; "I'm starting to get real tired Rick, it's way past my bedtime." He smiles as he leans toward me slapping my leg; "and for an old fart like you, it is really late." We laugh and he downs the last swallow.

"Ah, Dale? Would you... ah... would you sleep in my room tonight? I'll take the guest room. Just to see if they come back; and you... ah, see them."

"Oh sure." sarcasm dripping in his voice. "I see how it is, you want the boogey man to get me, is that it?" He laughs.

"I could only hope, and be rid of your sorry ass." I counter as we walk toward my bedroom. Getting serious, I say, "They often hover, or fly around the ceiling fan, and sometimes they lay in the bed with me.

"OOOH! That gives me a warm fuzzy!" Dale snickers. "So they may be in bed with me. Oh great! Goody goody gumdrops!" He laughs, lightly punching me on the arm. "Get out of here and leave me alone with your gremlins."

I return to the kitchen and finish my beer. Opening another, I sit at the kitchen table, listening for a sound from my bedroom. I wait through another beer before heading to the guest bedroom.

Dale said he was an early riser and when I came out to the patio at eight-forty he had made coffee, has his feet up on an adjoining chair reading the paper, enjoying the morning air. "Good morning!" He smiles cheerily as I open the door. "'bout time you get up. Sheesh. I was about to come in and see if you died. Damn! Do you sleep the day away or what."

"Allright! Allright! Gimme a break." We laugh.

After a while I get the courage to broach the subject, "So. How'd you sleep last night?"

In the process of taking a drink of coffee, he stops with a grunt. "Hunhh. I must admit, every time I got close to dozing off, I would turn and peek toward the fan for your buddies. At first the shadows played tricks on me but I realized it was the fan blades going around that I saw, and probably what you have been seeing as well." I didn't shake my head or offer an argument, but it is not the fan blades I see. "Other than that, I slept very well, thank you

– until almost six this morning. God, I haven't slept that late for a long time. I did get to see the sun come up though."

I offered him breakfast but he said he found cantaloupe in the refrigerator and that and the coffee was good enough. We relax on the patio; quietly watching groups of golfers pass by. Finally Dale starts slowly; "Have you thought about seeing a doctor?"

"Nope. I'm not sick."

"I didn't say you were but…"

"I'm not sick." I sternly interrupt.

"Rick. You have a lot on your mind, Kay's passing, Angel claiming much of your assets, who knows what tricks our minds play?"

"**I am not sick!**" I retort more vigorously.

He didn't say anything for a few minutes. "I know you are not sick, it's just that… my mother-in-law has seen some goofy things and the doctor gave her something that Diane keeps her on that makes her goofy things go away, maybe…"

I angrily turn on him, **"I AM NOT SICK!"**

"That's bullshit man!" Dale exclaims; "I might be able to see her getting half of everything Kay contributed to your assets, but Kay didn't work, never had to work. You put everything into the accounts. You earned everything. Why does Angel have the right to claim anything? Well, let me take that back, she should be entitled to get something from her mother having died, but good grief! Half? No way!"

I shrug. "My lawyer says there is nothing I can do but abide by the law."

"That law sucks." Dale sat deep in thought for a few minutes; "How's a guy supposed to keep what he worked many years for?"

We finish the day sitting around talking, laughing, enjoying one another's company, Dale does not bring up the doctor again. I grill steaks and serve baked potatoes for dinner, by necessity I became pretty adept in the kitchen during Kay's illness. Later we watch television and enjoy some quiet time while sipping on beer; "Ready for another?" I ask.

"Another! Good grief I've had, what..., seven beers today? That's more than I normally have in a month!" I feel somewhat guilty at having two beers to his one. "Rick I hate to admit it, but I am feeling tipsy, ha... tipsy my ass! I'm drunk!" Dale said, shaking his head. "It is only nine-twenty but I am winding down, very tired, I am not used to being up until way after midnight like we were last night." We say our goodnights and Dale retires to the guest bedroom.

Just before midnight I enter the guest bedroom and gently shake my friend; "Dale. Dale." I whisper. He looks at me startled. "They're in there now."

"OK. Let's go." He quickly got out of bed.

My heart sinks the moment we enter the bedroom. They are not sitting on the couch as they were before I woke Dale. He stares at the empty couch, even moving slightly for a different angle before he looks at me in dismay, "Rick?"

"I know." I raise my hands to a defensive position, move toward my bed and lift the pillows. Not there either. I look at him and shrug, "I know."

"It's obvious Rick, they don't want me to see them. They appear to you but... well shoot Rick? What can I say?" Dale is sincerely supportive.

By the sixteenth hole I comment to Dale, "I'm really tired."

"You should be! Damn, you take twice as many shots as I do! You're getting too easy. Haven't you been playing?"

"Nah, I can count on one hand the number of times I have been out the past two years. In Minnesota, well, Don doesn't play and Kay was not well and... and needed me, so I stayed around the house mostly."

"I've never seen you play so poorly." Dale counters softly; "We have always been fairly close in our scores, but today... well you have a lot of distractions, a lot on your mind." Then with a sly grin and a nudge continues; "What little mind there is."

Back at the house, we pop open a beer and make plans for dinner. "We don't have to go anywhere; we can just stay here and order a pizza or something." Dale offers.

"Pizza! Damn! I have had enough Pizza lately. Seems like I have a pizza every other day, nah, there is a burger joint down the road, we can go there, my treat."

"Well of course! Isn't that the price you pay for getting your butt whooped so badly in golf?"

The telephone interrupts our laughter. It is Monty Sterns. After initial pleasantries I stop talking and listen. Hanging up, I stare at Dale.

"What? What is it?" Dale's concern is evident, "What?"

The words Monty spoke stunned me. I can hardly repeat them. Leaning against the kitchen counter for support, I find the strength. "Angel has frozen my assets until the outcome of my competency hearing."

Chapter Six

Penguins! I hate these damn teenagers with their pants down below their butts, it's stupid! When they walk, they look like penguins, waddling around sticking their legs out to the side, grabbing their crotch to keep the pants from falling down. Just pull 'em up for Christ sake! Some have baseball caps turned to the side, some with hoodies over caps, others not. Hooded sweatshirts are pulled up over their heads, one with a cap on backwards hood down, most with wires coming from under the hood, must be those I-pods or something, I muse. Playing that rap crap no doubt, as they seem to be loosely keeping time with a barely discernible 'noise'. Yep! Just what I thought, rap crap. And it's not just a black issue for among the eight to ten kids milling about in front of the food court in the mall, are three white kids, penguins all.

As I push my way past them to enter the food court, my contempt boils over and I mutter; "Spear chuckers." Now where did that come from? I am not blatantly prejudiced. OK, maybe I do have some prejudiced leanings, but I am not a racist.

"WHA'CH'U SAY!" The nearest black boy yells at me. The others look at him, then at me. "WHA'CH'U SAY MOTHER FUCKER!" He yells again and starts toward me. One of the other boys grabs him by the arm. "HE CALL ME A SPEAR CHUCKER!" He exclaims loudly to his companions.

"What's going on here?" A man wearing a manager's pin on his lapel asks as he steps from behind the counter. He is short and portly, probably two hundred fifty pounds with puffy red cheeks and less than six foot tall. Perched on his head is a paper cap proclaiming the name of the establishment, Domino's Pizza. Wiping his hands on a dirty apron, he looks quizzically at the tall thin black boy.

"This mother f.."

"Whoa!" The manager quickly chops off the latter part of the black boys' sentence.

Pointing at me, the boy angrily says; "He call me a spear chucker!"

"Anything I can do to help?" A tall elderly mall security officer asks, having noticed the ruckus starting. It is time for me to leave.

"Hold that man." The manager directs the security officer, who holds up his hand to me. I stop. "Is that true sir?" The manager asks.

I shrug and turn my palms up non-committal, "I'm sorry." I offer sheepishly toward the boys.

"No he aint!" The tall African American boy yells pointing at me; "I want the son-of-a-bitch thrown in jail for… for… for sumpin'. I aint takin' shit from this honky bastard!"

"Calm down son, we'll take care of this. Come with me sir." The burly security officer said to me.

"I'm pressin' charges on 'im! I want you call da cops!"

"Yeah! We want da cops called to 'rest him!" One of the white boys chimes in; "We don't have to take his racist shit. We gonna be right here 'til we see's justice done." They look menacing. "You gonna call da fuckin' cops or what?"

"Calm down son." The security guard holds his hand up to the boys, then looks at the manager who nods.

The manager guides me to a table in a corner of the food court where my back is to the wall, while the security officer speaks with the boys. I watch the boys flail their arms about pointing at me while the guard listens intently. The manager positions himself between me and the conversations carried out near the doorway. The manager moves slightly closer to the group as the security guard nods and speaks into his hand held radio, then motions for the boys to follow him. I start to get up but the manager holds his hand out, indicating I should remain seated.

I feel like a little kid made to sit in the corner for being bad. Shoot I wasn't bad; I didn't mean anything by it.

It is kind of dark in this corner but a strange darkness, as it seems to move when I turn my head to see it. The darkness moves to the right when I turn my head to the right and to the left when I move my head to the left. Yep. It even moves upward when I look toward the ceiling. Not a complete darkness, just around the edges of my eyesight. Kind of like… well not a halo… what is it you call something that is just around the edges? Oh well, that's where the darkness is… just around the edges.

There is light, but it is a funny kind of light. The restaurant lights are in the ceiling, a single bulb visible in each circular hole in the ceiling. The light has… spokes (?) of light coming from the bulb. I stare at the light in wonder. I don't recall ever seeing light rays coming from a bulb before. It is like I can see the light start from the source in the bulb and go out to the far wall where it grows dark. Moving my head back and forth does not change the rays but does cause them to rotate slightly almost like bicycle spokes. Shaking my head does not dim the outline around my eyes. There is a shadow though, in front of me.

"Sir." The shadow speaks.

It is Barry, the food court manager. "Are you alright?"

I must have dozed off. Was I dreaming? I look at the lights, nearly blinded by the brightness.

The responding officer is a blonde haired cop that is very large, six and a half feet tall at least. He looks familiar. He listens intently to the security guard, the manager and group of kids, making notes on a small spiral notebook pulled from his breast pocket. After a while he came to the corner of the restaurant where I sit; "Let's go."

He keeps looking at me as he leads me to his patrol car. Finally he stops; "You look familiar, I've seen you before haven't I?"

I glance at him for a moment, and shrug.

He studies me momentarily, then asks; "By the golf course? You saw… had some… some strangers in your house?"

I still do have… wait! Is he the cop that came to my house? Yeah, I remember now! I nod.

He says nothing for a few minutes, having seated me in the back of the cruiser. Strangely, he does not start the patrol car but sits in silence, fumbling with a notebook. Suddenly, he turns and looks at me sternly; "Look, I'll make this go away; you go home and get yourself straight. You seem to be a decent sort, but if you so much as j-walk, both of our asses will be in a sling, understand?"

I am dumbfounded, unable to believe my ears. My doomed state is about to be lifted; a reprieve from an extremely embarrassing and potentially costly situation.

After thanking him profusely and assuring him I have learned a valuable lesson and am not a bigot, I still have a guilty feeling. He pointed at me and said; "Get it together."

I nod.

Chapter Seven

"I aint sick!" I defiantly stare at the doctor. HA! Doctor, that's a loose term for a shrink, but I guess society sees psychiatrists as doctors, although I don't believe in them. Someone for crazies to talk to and I am **not** crazy.

"No one says you are Mr. Hageman." The nattily dressed man says softly in reassuring tones. He is a man in his early fifties, perhaps late forties, slightly graying hair that almost touches the collar of his light brown turtleneck sweater in the back. He is thinner and taller than I, and looks more athletic.

His office is not stark, but plainly furnished with subdued lighting, not dark but neither is it bright, nothing distracting. There is a couch, but I am in a large, soft leather armchair, I squelch the urge to look for the lever that reclines the chair.

"You appear nervous Mr. Hageman." He continues. I snort, but do not respond. "We would like you to relax. We have been ordered by the court to speak with you, which is pretty much a formality in court cases. Usually we just enjoy pleasant conversations with the people they send us, but you wouldn't believe some of the people we have had to see. Oh the stories we could tell, I think we'll write a book after we get done with this shrink business." He states with a quick laugh. Hey, this guy is not half bad, although I wonder who the 'we' is. Am I going to talk to another, or does he refer to himself as 'we'.

"What about Doctor patient privileges?" I ask with a laugh.

"Yeah," he nods, "that may get in the way... but the stories we could tell... ah... well." He smiles and shakes his head.

We chat about nothing in particular for most of an hour, the weather, the Dallas Cowboys prospects for this season, where I grew up, family history and other things that do not strike me as pertinent to my court case. Finally he says, "Well this hour has passed quickly. We have enjoyed our meeting with you Rick." By now we are on a first name basis, although for me it is, Doctor Blake. "We must meet at least one more time, court orders you know." He smiles, "Day after tomorrow, same time?"

The second meeting with Doctor Blake is not unlike our first for several minutes, but he interjects questions about recent events and we discuss my 'guests', the bank, lawyers and the kids at the mall. Later, reflecting on our meeting, I am amazed at how we conducted small talk interspersed with details about my life and recent events. He offered such sincere condolences when we discussed Kay's passing, that he gave me the impression he felt the pain as if he had known her. Mostly he sat and listened as I opened up more than anticipated, but I guess that is what he is supposed to do... sneaky bastard.

"Well guess what?" I say with some apprehension to my 'friends' on the couch. "I told Doctor Blake all about you guys today. Now what do you have to say about that?" They don't look at me or respond, as if they are not there and I am talking to myself. "I think you would like him, he seems so much like we are, just a regular guy." I almost laugh at the 'we' part as if they and I are peers.

Back in the kitchen I open another beer and rummage in the refrigerator for something to eat. Maybe I'll go out tonight, nah; I'll just watch television.

The judge barely acknowledges the small gathering in the courtroom as he takes his seat on the bench and listens to the obligatory bailiff spiel. Why is it called a bench? It's more like a tall desk than a bench. You sit on a bench not at a bench. I snicker to myself. The 'bench' is in the left corner of the elongated courtroom with a witness chair to the judges left between the bench and a long jury box. There are no jurors in the box as this case is to be heard by the judge. Two tables front the judges' bench with my lawyer and I seated at the right hand table and Angel and her lawyer to our left.

Running my fingernail along the edge, I look around the table to see if any of the edges of the… what is it called, this type of top? It is just cheap wood or board covered with… Formica! That's it, Formica. Wow, couldn't come up with that term right away. Anyhow, I often see loose edges around Formica table tops. This one must be new. I peek around my attorney to catch a glimpse of Angel but she is blocked from my view by her attorney.

Now that son-of-a-bitch Doctor Blake, is telling everyone in clinical terms how I am bigoted, homophobic, and a delusional manic depressive. He is but one of a parade of witnesses to testify against me. Lance tells of how I shied away when he tried to initiate a friendly greeting. That lying homo bastard! I made the first contact, not him. The banker tells how I became unreasonably irate when he tried to explain legal issues regarding financial transactions after a death. Unreasonable, what is unreasonable about wanting to access my own money? The friendly police officer told me about my calling 911 and the intruder alert that turned out to be 'ghosts'.

The upshot is when two black kids I do not recognize, tell how I instigated a near altercation with my racist outcries against them. Jeez! They don't even look like the same spear chuckin' penguins I saw at the Mall. I laugh quietly. These two are neatly dressed in sport shirts and slacks pulled up to a normal position. They actually look like decent young men. And when they speak, it is not as if their mouth is full of marbles, but they sound articulate. Are these the same kids that wore hoodies, with their pants down around their thighs? Everything is blown out of proportion; they all make me sound... oh shit... bigoted, homophobic and delusional.

My lawyer, Mr. Watson, put up my probate lawyer Monty Sterns, my best friends Dave and Dale, Mike Walters the CEO of my former company and my daughter Dawn. All testify I am, and always have been, sane, rational and devoted to family and friends. Under cross examination they admit I changed after Kay's death but did not consider that unusual under the circumstances.

My lawyer instructed me early in the proceedings that my step daughter requested no contact with me during the hearing. That is alright with me, as we never got along anyway. But now the bitch… I should stop referring to her that way, wants to put me away for being crazy. It is an effort to get my entire assets. She was always a selfish and greedy bitch, not at all like her mother.

We sit on a bench outside the courtroom, (yes, a real wooden bench), Dave, Dale, Dawn and I, the testimony completed, discussing what had transpired. They offer support but, with concerned, worried expressions in their eyes and voices. My lawyer, Mr. Watson, has been conferring with Angel's attorney for at least an hour. Finally he comes from one of the side rooms along the corridor and approaches us.

"Mr. Hageman, your daughter-in-law will drop the competency suit." He began.

"YES!" Dave and Dale exclaim.

Mr. Watson holds up his hand. "There is a stipulation." We stare at him. "On the condition that you relinquish half your house and give her right of first refusal in the event you attempt to sell the property".

I reply, "Well I guess I can do that, I'll just stay in the house forever and the bitch will never get it." I state, eliciting uneasy laughter from my friends.

Mr. Watson is not amused. "There is more. She wants her mother's Lexus, two hundred and fifty thousand dollars and twelve thousand dollars annually for twenty years."

We are silent, stunned, until Dale whispers; "Holy shit!"

The wooden bench we waited in anticipation upon moments earlier; now seems extremely uncomfortable. "Mr. Watson, that's over half of my assets... Jesus!" I plead.

He looks at the floor. "Our options are this: We can refuse and try to get a favorable judgment in your competency hearing, which... I must be direct and honest with you. Your friends gave testimony about what you used to be like, whereas she has witnesses that testified to your present state of mind. It does not look good for a favorable judgment."

"Can I speak with her?" Dawn asks.

Mr. Watson pauses and looks at her silently for several moments. Detecting no anger, he asks, "For what purpose?"

Dawn looks down, then glances at me; "Angel and I have never been close and actually... well, I never have liked her but... he is my dad." She gently strokes my forearm. "I must try to rationalize with her."

Mr. Watson looks at me. "What do you think?" I shrug. With no other response, he motions to Dawn, "Let's give it a shot." The two of them walk toward the side room he came from earlier. Out of earshot, they face each other in discussion, getting their strategy down I surmise.

More than thirty minutes pass before the two of them come from the side room, Mr. Watson smiling, Dawn has been crying, her eyes puffy and red.

"Well, she did it!" The lawyer exclaims casting an admiring glance in Dawn's direction. "She got her to come off her high handed demands and settle for much less."

I stand and hug her tightly. Dave and Dale enthusiastically express their appreciation.

I look at Mr. Watson and ask, "How much less?"

"She wants the same deal for the house, the right of first refusal and approval of any sale. Also the Lexus, and two hundred thousand dollars with no annual."

"Wow!" I sink back to the bench. "That is still very steep."

"Yes, it is steep, but less than thirty percent of your cash assets and she had been demanding more than half of what you have."

"Is this my best option?"

"I think it is." He answers.

Chapter Eight

Perhaps it is only the dark, dreary cold day that makes me feel so down. No, more than down, am I angry? I don't know, yeah maybe I do feel angry. It's after Christmas and before New Years and Kay hasn't been talking to me. Of course I don't expect her friends to say anything; they hadn't acknowledged me since they came a few months ago. They sit on the couch in my bedroom but Kay has been lying with me in bed for a few weeks now, although we have not... we have not... well she seems to be a bit distant, somewhat disinterested in me, so we haven't...

Christmas was a great day, Kay and I exchanged presents, although she has not opened the gift I bought her, and her just being here is present enough for me, it's ok that she didn't get me anything. Dawn pleaded with me to join her for Christmas but I begged off claiming to not feel well. I would much rather spend the holiday with Kay than anyone else. Dawn doesn't understand why I would not share the day with them. I did not try to explain about Kay, Dawn wouldn't understand.

Now I look at the cold grey sky reflecting on the argument Kay and I had last night. Cold? Well the sky is grey, but cold? I laugh as I recall days in Minnesota after Christmas and how this fifty-six degree temperature would be considered downright balmy this time of year there. Yeah, I guess it is all relative.

Relative, ha, or relatives, is what the argument was about last night. I asked Kay if the people with her are relatives of hers and who they are, but she would not answer me. They appeared to get angry as my voice rose trying to get Kay to respond. They moved around much faster as if agitated and growled, bringing a greater sense of apprehension to me. At least now they do not ignore me, but I feel more threatened and fearful, especially from the pointy nosed bastard who takes exception to my arguing with Kay. He gives me the creeps with his sneering at me.

Sipping on my beer, I reflect on our argument, still angered that she will not tell me who these people are. She, and they, went somewhere today which is not at all like her to run away from a confrontation. She always faced up to our differences before she… before she… died? Gotta get that thought out of my head as she has been here with me the past few weeks, so she is not… aw shit! She'll come back. I'll show her. When she comes back I won't talk to her, then she'll know what it's like to have someone barely pay attention to you. And… and… and her 'friends' can growl and snarl at me all they want, I won't pay attention to them either.

"911, what's your emergency?" The operator intones.

"I have four of them sons-a-bitches holed up in my garage at gunpoint, they can't get out."

"Do they have guns sir?" She asks.

I whisper into the phone, "I don't see any but... HEY! HEY! GET BACK!"

"Are they threatening you sir? I'll have a team there immediately."

"They seem threatening, they moved, but I have them under control for now." I say before giving the address.

The front door opens, assuming it is the police, "BACK HERE!" I yell from the garage toward the front door. The sound of shuffling feet tell me they are coming down the hallway and will soon come into the garage.

"DROP THE GUN! PUT THE GUN DOWN!" The officer yells as I look over my shoulder at them.

"But I've got them covered so they can't escape!" I plead turning partly toward the officer.

"BACK! DOWN! PUT THE GUN DOWN! We will take care of things." He states as he cautiously approaches, gun leveled at me. "Put it down. Put it down."

"Damn!" I say as the gun drops to my side. He quickly grabs the weapon from my hand and presses me against the wall. "Hey!" I exclaim as pain shoots up my arm pinned against my back. "You're hurting me! They're getting away! You're letting them escape! Stop them! Stop them!" They don't listen, but place handcuffs on my wrists. "What are you doing? What... what! It's them, not me! Leave me be!"

"Calm down, take it easy, everything is alright, calm down. See anything Roger?" The officer asks his partner. 'Roger' looks around the garage, "Nope."

"Of course not you idiots, you let them escape!" I growl through clenched teeth.

"No one got past us sir. The garage door and windows are closed, so no one can get out."

"You dumb shits, they don't need an open door to get out, they just go through the doors or the walls… and you let them. I had them contained but you assholes let them get away!"

The officers do not speak for a moment, until the second man says quietly, "I'll call it in."

It is uncomfortable in the back seat of their patrol car, hands cuffed behind my back, my arms hurt at the shoulders and I adjust in the seat to find the least painful position. The officers are filling out paperwork in the front seat, the police radio blaring messages. The passenger side officer suddenly reaches for the microphone and speaks, "Roger dispatch, The Oasis." His partner nods, puts down his paperwork and backs out of my driveway.

"Where the hell are we going?" I ask sternly. The officer on the passenger side glances toward me without response. I catch the driver's eye in the mirror but he also does not respond. Quiet types I muse. Oh well, might as well sit back and, ahem, 'enjoy' the ride.

I try to determine where we are headed, but do not recognize the streets or landmarks we pass. We ride for… five minutes, ten minutes, I don't know how long until we pass through gates attached to ten foot high brick walls. What is this place? Proceeding up the long circular drive, we pass several people seated on chairs or benches.

I laugh as an older man in white pajamas waves his arms about, dancing on the grass. Crazy sombitch. Other men and women, mostly elderly, sit on benches enjoying the sunshine, or slowly walk around the grounds. A small pond surrounded by colorful flowers is in the center of the grounds. Nurses tend to, or watch the people. A man in white pants and jacket walks beside a nurse in a white uniform and nurse's cap, as they approach a group sitting in the shade. Is this a hospital?

The patrol car stops in front of a white Colonial style building set well back from the street. Four columns on the veranda, focus attention to oversized double doors with the large lettering "The Oasis" over them. Through the doors briskly walks a middle aged woman in a grey pant suit followed by two large men in white uniforms. The woman holds a clipboard pressed lightly to her hip and the two men, one black and one white, stand solemnly behind her. Both men, over six feet tall and close to three hundred pounds, are imposing figures. They look very stern.

The trio approaches the patrol car and the woman addresses the officer, "Officer Renquist?"

"Yes." The officer on the passenger side responds, opens the back door, grabs my arm and gives a gentle tug, "Come with us Mr. Hageman." The large men in uniforms take hold of my arms as I step out of the cruiser.

"Sign here officer Renquist." The woman says, and he signs where indicated. "We will take it from here, thank you." Pleasant bitch isn't she I think as the uniformed men usher me inside.

"Where are you taking me?" I ask politely.

They say nothing and lead me to a small office with a desk cluttered with papers, a computer monitor on the right side. "Sit here." the white officer says gruffly, pushing me toward the chair in front of the desk.

"OK! Thank you very much!" I say dryly.

A couple of minutes pass before the grey clad lady comes into the room and sits behind the desk. She is neither unattractive nor very pretty. In her mid to late fifties, hair pulled back in a bun, or whatever that style is called. There are grey streaks in hair that otherwise is a light brown. "Oh Jeannie with the light brown hair" I smile recalling an old song. Nah, a song doesn't fit her; I wonder who she is and what I am doing here.

"Mr. Hageman, do you know why you are here?" She begins.

"I don't even know where here is?" I counter.

"OK, yes, I'm sorry. Well, 'here' is 'The Oasis' a state run facility that deals with emotional issues and patients that exhibit a propensity for violence and …."

"Whoa! Wait just a goddamned minute there." I began to rise up out of the chair but am quickly pushed down by the two, ahem, gentlemen. There is nothing gentle about how they plant me back into the chair.

Composing myself, I continue in a quieter tone. "What I mean to say is that I am not a violent person and have never…"

"Did you have a gun?" She cuts me off.

"Well, yes but…"

"And did the officers have to take it away from you and handcuff you?"

"Well no, I mean I would have given it to them if they asked, but..."

"And were you holding other people at bay with the pistol?"

"They would have tried to get away if I didn't stop them, but the police just let them go without trying to stop them!"

A pretty Nurse in a white uniform, a white cap perched atop her pony tailed red hair; enters holding a small paper cup. "Here is what you asked for Mrs. Mallon." and set the cup on the edge of the desk near the computer monitor.

Mrs. Mallon types on the computer, leans back and looks at the young nurse. "Also get this for me Jacki." turning the screen toward the young nurse who reads the message and departs. "Harvey." she continues, "Get Mr. Hageman a glass of water."

"Yes'm." The large black attendant whirls about. In a matter of seconds he returns and places a large styrofoam cup in front of Mrs. Mallon.

"Mr. Hageman, I want you to take these with this water." She shows me the smaller cup with five pills in it, two large white pills, one small blue, one small green, and one medium sized white pill.

"I don't want any pills." I start.

"Yes, Mr. Hageman, you do, it is for your own good. Take them."

"Nah. I don't want to."

"It's for your own good sir."

"Nope. Don't want any." I say defiantly.

She looks at the men behind me. "Would you prefer Harvey and Wayne assist you in taking the pills?"

"They can take the pills and shove 'em up their ass for all I care. They are not going to make me take any pills I don't want."

Oh, how wrong I am. They roughly take me out of the chair, wrestle me to the floor and, while one holds me, the other grips my chin squeezing my cheeks against my teeth, forces my mouth open and inserts the pills. I try to spit them out, but he catches them, forcefully pushing them back into my mouth and pours water into my mouth before I can spit again.

"Swallow!" The black man yells as he holds my mouth shut. I almost choke and have no choice but to swallow them in order to breathe again. As soon as I swallow, he yanks my mouth open and peers inside. "He swallowed 'em ma'am."

I cough violently gasping for breath as I look hatefully at the behemoths.

"Now Mr. Hageman, we want you to be cooperative during your stay here. There will be medication administered and it will be much better if you did not resist. We don't want any more trouble do we?" The condescending bitch.

The two behemoths help me to my feet and place me in the chair as the young nurse returns with another small cup. Mrs. Mallon looks at me with a knowing smile.

"Now Mr. Hageman, we aren't going to have a scene with this one are we?"

Still coughing and breathing heavily, I contemplate what will happen if I refuse, glance at the huge attendants and take the cup she extends toward me. "The water too, Mr. Hageman." Oh isn't she sweet.

"Dad! Dad!" The voice is distant yet vaguely familiar. "Dad!" There it is again, oh, I don't have my eyes open. There is light but only a fog as I try to press my eyes open and pick my head up. My head is heavy, spinning round and round, so I let it remain on the pillow. "Daddy." The voice is closer. I squint and blink several times to bring the form into focus. I recognize the voice and try to speak her name, damn, my lips are heavy and no sound comes out.

"Oh daddy, I got here as soon as I could, they called last night, asking several questions, would not let me come last night, but I am here now and will get you out of here as soon as I can."

"Mmmm ... pht..." I mumble feebly.

"Are you alright, dad?"

"UNH ... wha 'm ... mmm pht." My mouth and lips will not move, stuck together.

"Dad? Can you hear me? Open your eyes dad. Open your eyes daddy! Are you alright?"

What did she say? "M mmm a ..." The words do not come out right and I force my mouth open. Things a little less fuzzy now. "... Wha...?"

"This place is called 'The Oasis' and they put people here that are… are violent or… criminal… or insane." The last words are whispered.

Exerting considerable effort, I try to sit up in bed, but am very dizzy and fall back against the pillow. Through the haze I note a large dormitory style room. Several beds line the walls on both sides of an aisle. Although surely not an accurate count, there are perhaps ten beds on each wall with dormant shapes of men on each bed. There may be more as the room is very large. I'll be sure to count when my eyes clear. Oh shit! The Neanderthal is here! The big black bastard!

"AAH'N aah." I mumble feebly pointing a limp finger in his direction. He looks at me but does not move or blink an eye. Dawn follows my gaze, looking at the large attendant behind her. He does not acknowledge her, but keeps his arms folded across his massive chest.

Dawn helps me sit up on the edge of the bed, and turns to the big man, "Would you ask Mrs. Mallon to come here?" He looks at her. "Sir?" Dawn continues, and stares at the big man. He reluctantly pulls a radio from his hip and speaks quietly into it.

Dawn asks me, "Where are your clothes?"

A hospital gown hangs loosely around me barely maintaining my modesty. I reach toward the back but fall backward onto the bed. Dawn tries, but cannot hold me up. "Let me help you dad."

I shake my head to decline but it spins as though it will fall off. Damn, I am weak, can't hold myself up. What is going on?

Dawn asks again. "Where's your clothes dad?"

"M..mmm...ere?" I weakly point under the bed.

Dawn glances down and looks at me as she shakes her head. "Nothing there dad. Don't you have a jacket like that one?" She points to an unkempt old man on the other side of the dorm, "Sir?" Dawn began to walk toward the old man in a beige jacket.

"WHOA THERE!" The Neanderthal yells, quickly cutting her off. "No! No! No! You cain't go over dere!"

"But he has..."

"You gots to stay by yo' father, cain't go no foother." He says, cutting short her protest.

"But he has my dad's jacket. That man over there!" Dawn indicates the old man wearing the light beige colored jacket.

"No he don't."

"What?" Dawn can't believe he is denying it.

"I say he don't got yo' dad's jacket." The attendant said with eyes glaring.

"But..."

"HEY! OL MAN! Whose dat jacket yo' wearin'?"

The old man shuffles off holding tightly onto the jacket.

Dawn will not take no for an answer insisting, "That is my dad's jacket, I bought it for him."

"He gots his name in it?" The huge attendant asks with a toothy grin.

"Well that's pretty juvenile. What adult writes his name on his clothes?" She states sarcastically to the stone wall.

A pretty young nurse enters carrying a small paper cup and nods pleasantly toward Dawn, then steps alongside my bed. "Sit up now sir." She begins, placing her hand behind my back to assist me up.

"What are you giving him?" Dawn asks sharply.

"Don' you go botherin' nurse Jacki none ma'am." The ape speaks sharply.

"It's OK Harvey." The nurse says softly, lifting me into an upright position. "It is his prescribed medication; the last dosage apparently wore off so we have been directed to increase the frequency."

"But what is it?"

Nurse Jacki smiles at Dawn, "You will have to take that up with Dr. Mallon. She is in charge of his case."

"Can I at least get his jacket back? And where are the rest of his clothes?"

"Sorry Miss, I don't know what you are referring to."

I become afraid for my father, and have the impression he is not getting the care one desires for a family member. There is no evidence of abuse, at least physical abuse, yet he cannot speak, or hold himself up, his strength sapped. I suspect he has been drugged so heavily that he can't hold his head up. He is not yet sixty-five years old and should not be in this condition.

Doctor Mallon is seated at her desk as Nurse Jacki ushers me in. Looking from the nurse to me, the Doctor rises, extends her hand with a smile, "What can I do for you Mrs. Scott?"

"I am concerned for my father. He isn't very responsive, can't seem to speak or move."

"Nothing to worry about." The Doctor smiles. "Take a seat." She politely indicates the chair in front of her desk. "Many new patients take some time to adjust to their medication, it's nothing unusual. He will adjust; some take as long as a couple of weeks and, in rare cases, up to a month to become acclimated to their regimen."

"Well you don't have to worry about that as I am taking him out of here today. You won't need to medicate him any further."

She looks at me quizzically for a moment before saying; "Mrs. Scott, your father has been committed to this institution. He cannot go home with you today, or any day. He is our patient."

My shock must be evident as I cannot find a voice to speak. All of a sudden the clothing issue diminishes greatly in importance.

"Surely you must have expected this when your father threatened the police, had to be restrained and subdued as a danger to the police and those around him. He cannot be allowed to endanger others. This is the place for him... and others like him."

"He has been committed without a hearing or notification of his next of kin? You can't do that."

"Mrs. Scott, I understand your concern for your father, but the State of Texas must look after the welfare of all its citizens and cannot make exceptions for one individual. I'm sorry but the paperwork is in."

My mind races frantically. "Paperwork, has his commitment been finalized?"

"Well technically it takes a couple of days to process the paperwork for him to become a ward of the State. That should happen tomorrow, or the next day or two for certain. There's nothing you can do."

"Mrs. Scott, I will set a meeting with Judge Barlow this afternoon." Mr. Watson tells me in haste. "We don't have much time if what you are telling me is true. Let me put in a call for the Judge, after which I'll contact the institution to see if I can reason with them. Gloria!" He spoke into an intercom.

"Yes sir."

"Start researching commitment laws and find a reason for releasing my client, Rick Hageman, to his daughter, Dawn Scott."

"I am on the Silver case right now sir, should I give that to someone else?" The voice on the intercom responds.

" No. Set that aside for now. This has priority."

"Yes sir. I am on it."

He picks up the telephone and punches some numbers. "Cameron, I need a favor. Can you get me a meeting with your dad this afternoon? Yes, this afternoon, as early as possible. It is of vital importance that I meet with him ASAP." He listens intently as he peers at me. "Thanks Cam, I await your call." He replaces the telephone in its cradle.

"Cameron Barlow." Mr. Watson responds to my puzzled looks. "He is a lawyer friend and son of Judge

Barlow. Don't worry Dawn; I will do everything I can to make this right for your father."

"He is not a criminal and he is not crazy." I plead.

"I know he is not. He is just going through a rough stretch right now. Keep your chin up, everything will turn out alright."

Dad's lawyer from the commitment trial, Mr. Watson, works feverishly on dad's situation and, having his attempt to reason with "The Oasis" rebuffed, is able to secure a temporary injunction against commitment until Judge Barlow can review the case.

Before we enter Judge Barlow's chambers, Mr. Watson turns to me, "Let Gloria and I attend to this matter. No, it's alright." He smiles as I begin to protest. "What goes on behind closed doors stays behind closed doors." He says with a wink.

Twenty minutes later, Gloria and Mr. Watson come toward me with big smiles. "The clerk is drawing up the paperwork. It should not be much longer and you will be able to take him home with you."

"How did you... how did..." I stammer.

He smiles and winks at me.

The Doctors in the emergency ward at the Denton Hospital examine Dad and review the medication list the Judge ordered supplied by "The Oasis". "Mrs. Scott, your father has been given some very aggressive medication and, perhaps an abundance of it. Much of the medication is designed to sedate him, or keep him quiet."

"Fast aint he." I declare faintly.

Dawn looks at me. "What?"

"Fast." I motion toward the horses.

Dawn glances in the rear view mirror. "Yes, they are." She is almost oblivious to the cavorting horses.

Dawn honks the horn as we pass the horse barn. Chad rises up from his chore and waves. He is a good son-in-law, provides well for my daughter and grandson. Nice guy, doesn't act like a rich man, very down to earth, not snooty like some.

As we approach the main house, Jeff waves running toward the house. Good boy. He is nearly out of breath as his mother helps me out of the car. "Hey, grandpa!" He greets me excitedly.

I smile and nod weakly toward him.

"Help me with your grandpa, Jeff."

To my amazement, my legs are weak and my head swims dizzily. With assistance from Jeff and Dawn, I traverse the many steps to the second floor and proceed down the hall toward one of the guest rooms. Dawn told me I would be staying with her but did not say for how long.

"Jeff, did you get the things from dad's house like I asked you?"

"Yes Mom, I think I got everything."

"Well, if you didn't, we can pick some things up at the store. Daddy, sit here, shall I turn on the TV?" I nod weakly.

The guest room is approximately forty foot square with a walk-in closet and large bathroom off to one side.

Dawn seats me in a recliner, the door to the bathroom/closet to my right, the entry door behind me; in front a flat screen television is on the wall. To my left is a love seat with a small end table on its left side. Adjacent to the television and centered on the forty foot wall is a door flanked by windows that leads to the deck outside the guest room. Opposite the deck door is a king size bed and dresser. On the space to the left of the deck door is a mini-bar with a stereo system and bookcase on the wall behind it. It is a very luxurious room. Kay and I have been here before.

Dawn came from the closet and said, "I think Jeff has picked up enough clothes for you to be comfortable. He placed your shaving gear, toothbrush and other stuff on the shelf in the bathroom. If you need anything else you will let me know won't you?" I nod. "Good. Here is the remote for the television; I'll be back to check on you in a little while."

The little while is like an eternity as I am stuck watching some God awful soap opera. I thought about getting up and at least turning off the damned TV but felt too weak to stand up. Finally she returns and asks, "How you doing dad?"

"Umph!" I mutter and point at the TV.

"You want something else on?" I nod. "Why didn't you change the channel?" She asks with a hint of exasperation. "You have the remote."

I motion with my hands palms up and grunt.

"Dad, I gave you the remote, it's right here beside you! All you have to do is press this button and it will go through the channels until you get to one you want to watch. See, this button, this one right here."

Sheesh! Now she tells me. "OK."

"Do you need to go to the bathroom or anything?" She is calmer now.

"Yes." I nod. She takes my arm and helps me to my feet. My strength is returning as I do not need as much assistance as a couple of hours earlier. It is only a few steps to the bathroom and she closes the door behind me. I wobble but maintain my balance.

None of my 'friends' are here, but neither is Kay. The room is comfortable, but after four days I still am not at ease here. My home may be lonely, but it is my home and if I am there perhaps Kay will return. I am certain it is the unfamiliar surroundings that's keeping her away.

"I want to go home." I state that night at dinner.

Dawn pauses, her fork still in her mouth. Sitting upright, she sets her fork down and dabs at her mouth with a napkin before responding, "You are at home daddy." She glances at Chad for reassurance.

He echoes his wife's assertion as he leans back, "You're welcome here, dad. You're family. If there is anything you need, just ask." I do not doubt his sincerity.

"Thanks, but I want to go to my home."

"We will talk about this later." Dawn lowers her eyes.

"What's to talk about, I'm going home and if I have to walk, then... I'll walk."

"Daddy, please don't be like this." She says softly, leaning over to touch my hand.

"Like what? It is a simple thing. Just load me up in the car and take me home. What else is there to talk about." I pull my hand away.

Chad wipes his mouth, clears his throat, and speaks, "Dad, we tried to make everything as comfortable for you here as possible. Please, we want you to consider this your home. If there is something we overlooked... well, we won't know what it is unless you tell us."

How can I tell them about Kay, how it is her I want to be with. I look at my hands and mutter, "You don't understand."

The sun is shining brightly, the temperature in the mid nineties, typical for mid June as we park in my driveway. I spent two miserable weeks at Dawn's place, perhaps more miserable for them than me as I became increasingly difficult for them. We battled nearly every night at the dinner table until they finally relent and agree to take me home.

"Are you sure you will be OK, dad?" Dawn asks as she helps me with my bags.

"Yep! Everything will be great now." I assure her.

Remaining for almost an hour, she arranges the things purchased at the grocery store, filling my shelves and refrigerator. I peek in my bedroom but no one is there yet. My excitement rises as I anticipate Dawn's departure, and Kay's arrival.

All afternoon and into the evening I check the couch in my bedroom to no avail. Finally I lay down on the bed. Turning quietly, I smile and say, "Well. It's about time you came back."

Sheesh, I am tired, my body aches. Damn, it's hell to get old! I can barely move my legs as I ease them over the side of the bed. What time is it? My back aches and I am stiff and sore. Sheesh, nearly nine O'clock. I'm usually up around eight in the morning, showered and dressed for the day. I must like to sleep more.

I sit on the 'john' with my elbow on my knee, and chin nestled in the palm of my hand wondering why I feel so tired. My legs have fallen asleep so I must have been sitting here for some time. Damn, gotta get up! Screw the shower, I'm hungry. Trudging to the kitchen, I pull on my robe and contemplate what to have for breakfast. There is plenty of Cantaloupe and I like that. I'll make a pot of coffee and have… oh shit! The Cantaloupe is sitting on the table, and is… dark, not orange colored. It is warm, or at least room temperature, and slimy to the touch. Shit, I must have forgotten to put it back in the refrigerator yesterday. Wow! I didn't think it would turn this dark overnight. It is almost black around the edges. I'm throwing that shit out.

Coffee, that'll perk me up. The coffeemaker is still on from the previous day and the last half inch on the bottom of the pot is very dark and smells bad. Pretty thick too as I pour it out and rinse the pot. I open the refrigerator door deciding to have cereal instead of Cantaloupe. No milk? Damn, there it is on the counter. It's warm too, and stinks! Damn, what the hell, am I getting forgetful? Gotta throw that out too.

Cinching my robe around my waist, I slip on my bedroom slippers and shuffle out to get the paper. Shuffle! I used to have a spring in my step but now can't seem to get my feet moving very fast. Beautiful day though, bright sun, birds singing, cars slowly pass by on the street outside the development.

Whoa! Why are there five papers in the driveway? One is enough! Is someone throwing extra papers in my driveway? Now I have to clean up this mess! One of the papers is nearly twice the size of the others; are these not all from the same day? This is a dilemma. As I return to the kitchen, a cursory inspection reveals each paper has a different picture on the front so they must not have been dumped by unkind neighbors. As I open the papers I take notice of the dates, the big paper is from Sunday July 27, and the most recent Tuesday July 29. HOLY COW! I have not picked up my papers for five days! What the hell is going on?

The hunger pangs nearly overwhelm me as I pull into a Perkins for breakfast, having given up on finding something at home. Not bothering to shower, I put on faded blue jeans and a pullover sweatshirt although it is quite warm. As I am shown to my booth I do not remove my cap for I did not bother to comb my hair either, getting lazy I guess. I always take off my cap indoors, but then again, I 'always' comb my hair... and shower in the morning.

"Coffee sir?"

"Yes please."

"Regular or decaf?" She asks politely, setting a cup on the table in front of me.

"Regular. This is Tuesday isn't it?"

"All day." She replies cheerily. "Shall I give you a couple minutes to look over the menu?"

"Sure. Yes please." OK it is Tuesday. The last day I remember was Wednesday, or was it Thursday, damn... I don't know any more. Menu, where... oh, right in front of me. What do I like? I'll just have some eggs and hash-browns, hmmm, which item is that? All the items have special names; none just say eggs and hash-browns. Maybe I'll just tell my waitress what I want. Which one is my waitress? Shit, I forgot already? That one is not looking at me, wait, here comes one that is looking at me.

"Have you decided?" She asks cheerily as she stops beside my booth.

"Ah, um yes, can I just have two eggs and hash-browns?" I ask tentatively.

"Sure. Would you like some ham or sausage with that?"

"Sausage please."

"Links or patties?"

"Patties. And some toast also."

"White, Wheat or Sourdough?"

"Wow. White I guess." Damn, so many decisions, so much to think about, too much to think about.

Chapter Ten

I casually glance toward the woman seated at the bar five stools down. She has a glass of wine and I catch her eye in the mirror behind the bar briefly. She is in her mid-fifties, as are most of the people frequenting this bar. I have been coming here for a couple of weeks, but this is the first time I recall seeing her. Her dark wavy hair just touches her shoulders and from this angle, she is quite good looking. Her tight fitting blouse and a short skirt accentuate a trim figure of a woman much younger than fifty; she wears her age well.

Picking up my glass of beer, I gather courage and stand up. She is sipping her wine and looking at the mirror behind the bar. Our eyes meet for a moment in the mirror before I approach her. The female bartender is busily washing glasses and casts a glance toward me saying something to the woman, and moves off.

"Hello." I say politely, "May I?" indicating the stool beside her.

She looks at me and smiles, "Yes, of course."

"Come here often?" Oh jeez! What an idiot! What a horrible line with which to break the ice. Surely you can think of something that does not sound as if you think she is a barfly.

"No, actually this is only the second time I have been here. I stopped in for a few minutes about a week ago and… I think I remember you were here then, about a week ago?"

"Yes! Yes, I believe I was!" I could have been.

"I thought I saw you."

Suddenly I feel more at ease and we enter into light, comfortable conversation. Several other people are in the place, some enjoying dinner at one of the eight tables on the opposite side of the planters dividing the bar and small dining area. The dining area is more brightly lit than the bar that had been nearly empty, but now has fifteen patrons seated before it. There are an additional five or six patrons standing behind the mostly male fifty something crowd around the bar.

It is difficult to hold a conversation amid the laughter and revelry the patrons share. Ignoring the others, the dark haired beauty and I share a few more drinks. The evening crowd slowly dwindles down and we share the space with two others at the far end of the bar. The male patron standing at the bar, leans on his right arm facing the female seated beside him. He laughs loudly and often while she tosses her hair back with a soft laugh. Finally they leave together and I wonder if I will ask this lady to come home with me. Alternately formulating the words to ask her to accompany me home, and how to say good night, I notice it is after midnight. Surely Kay will not take kindly to my having relations with another woman. My fears are allayed when my dark haired companion indicates she has to be home with her ailing mother soon. Whew! Now I won't have anything to explain to Kay.

106

"Hi Rick." The woman exclaims as she takes the stool next to mine.

I see something familiar about her, the dark hair, the trim delectable figure, but... wait! At this bar... the other night, of course... what is her name?

"Hi!" I smile eagerly. "What are you drinking?"

The smile fades slightly but quickly brightens, "You remember. You bought me several Cabernets the other night. More than I should have had, I think you were trying to take advantage of me." She smiles coyly.

I laugh uneasily. Advantage, how do I respond to that? No, I don't remember, but there is no reason to tell her that. I turn to the bartender, "Another beer and a Cabernet for... ah... the beautiful lady." What is her name? My pause must have been too obvious. She looks quizzically at me as she lights her cigarette. "You smoke?" Oh shit! Now she really is looking at me funny.

"Of course I smoke, don't you remember telling me how it stunted your growth and that I am too young to smoke?"

Damn! Why don't I remember that conversation? I vaguely remember her; perhaps her name will come to me as we sit here for a while.

"Here you go Rick." Even the lady bartender knows my name but I haven't seen her before, or have I?

"Thank you." Sheesh. Did the bartender hear... what's her name... address me? Is that how she knows my name?

"How's your mom Helen." The bartender addresses the woman.

Helen! Whew, Helen, that's her name. Thank God the bartender said her name as I had not yet come up with it.

"Thanks for asking, Helen."

"Wow! Both of you are named Helen?" I am met with stunned silence from both women.

"Rick?" The Helen beside me begins, her eyes searching mine as the bartender Helen moves to another customer. "Are you alright? We sat here, the three of us, having a great time, just a couple of days ago, surely you haven't forgotten?"

"Of course not." I lie. "I... just remarked it ... well it is kind of unusual for two... the two of you to have the same first name. That is quite a coincidence."

"You said the same thing two days ago." She says quietly.

"Well... it is... a coincidence, that is."

The rest of the evening is spent in pleasant conversation, my initial confusion forgotten. As the time slips quickly by, I began to feel uneasy about the eventual outcome for the evening. My fears are set aside as she mentions her mother. I walk her out to her car where she stops and gives me a quick kiss before getting in. Opening her window she says, "See you Saturday?" I nod woodenly. I wanted the kiss to have lingered much longer, or for us to have... well... taken the next step.

"Hi Rick." She said putting her arm around my shoulders and planting a warm kiss on my cheek.

"Hello… you." I recognize her but, damn… what's her name?

"Helen." She responds to my pause.

"Of course, I know that. How could I forget after that nice little kiss you gave me in the parking lot?"

She hesitates as she sits and straightens her skirt. Looking at me, she pauses before saying demurely, "Not to mention the time we had at your house."

What! What we had at my house? I don't remember anything at my house… did she… did we? God why don't I… why wouldn't I remember if we… ? Damn!

She pulled my face toward her and gave me a long kiss on the cheek. "You were great, you… you man you." and smiles as she stares into my blank eyes.

"Humph!" I laugh meekly, not feigning embarrassment, I am embarrassed. How should I respond? I motion for the bartender. "The usual please."

"Which is?" He asks.

Helen fumbles with a cigarette from her purse as she waits for me to respond; finally she says, "A Cabernet for me and a Coors Light for Rick." After lighting her cigarette, she asks. "Rick, are you OK, you seem forgetful." She smiles.

"Nah. I'm alright… just got something caught in my throat for a moment, couldn't speak." I lie.

At the end of the evening as we get up to leave, she leans against me, "I'll follow you home… again."

Again? I nod obligingly. I drive home much slower than usual to ensure she doesn't lose sight of me. Have we played this follow me home game before?

It is no use. Whether it is the thought of Kay or whatever... I could not perform for... for... Helen, that's her name. We lay together for a time before she gets up and begins to dress. "It's OK. I understand." She says trying to make me feel better. "Perhaps next time."

Oh good! She's saying there will be a next time.

I answer the doorbell soon after eight in the morning. "Hi Rick!" A man in his mid-fifties addresses me. "Here, I'll show you what I was talking about the other day." and he steps away from the door. When I do not follow he looks at me and motions, "Over here Rick. Let me show you what we were talking about, what needs to be taken care of."

What we were talking about? I have never seen this man before, but he seems to know me, had I... obediently I move outside and look up to where he is pointing.

"You see how those shingles are darker than others. Wind has lifted the shingles and water has gotten under them. The wood roofing is rotting and must be replaced." He said in an authoritative manner.

I look in the direction he is pointing and can barely make out discoloration in the shingles. "That's a problem?" I ask.

"A problem? You bet it is! We discussed that. I have your estimate here that you said you would sign when I brought it out today. You told me two days ago that you would sign." He sounds exasperated.

"I did?" Why don't I remember talking to him. Damn! I am getting so forgetful.

"I have it right here." He holds out a shiny aluminum clipboard/case, opens it and places an official looking computer generated form under the clasp. "Sign right here." Indicating the bottom of the page extended toward me.

I take the case and look at the paper. Should I sign this? I look at him.

"Right here, the line highlighted in yellow."

"But…"

He points to the line where I was to sign.

I sign.

A loud thumping and ripping sound on the roof awakens me and I discover a crew of men tearing off shingles and throwing them in a dumpster parked in my driveway.

"What's going on?" I demand loudly.

Three of the four Mexicans on the roof pause momentarily and look at me as a fourth continues tearing up shingles. A fifth man on the ground addresses me in broken English. "We… do what… we are told… senor. We… take off old… put on new."

"You're tearing up my roof?"

"Si Senor." He pulls a folded pink piece of paper from his pocket. "Our… eh… work order." I recognize my signature on the bottom. Did I authorize this and not remember it?

I return to the house and open a beer, perplexed about what is going on.

Watching manual labor always has held me transfixed. Not handy myself, I admire those who do quality work and these Mexicans look like they are good at putting on shingles, slapping on layer after layer, securing them with air powered staplers.

A man approaches, glancing at my roof then at me. He is younger, perhaps forty-ish, about my height, but sturdily built with a barrel chest and massive tanned arms.

"Howdy neighbor." He smiles as he extends his hand. "D.J. Forbes here."

"Rick Hageman." I answer.

"Quite a project you've got going on here." He points toward the workers.

"Yeah, they do good work… for Mexes." I laugh.

He chuckles uneasily, then after a pause, "Well, actually I find the 'Mexes' are good conscientious workers, I have several on my crews."

"Your crews?"

"Yes. I own a road construction company and well over half my employees are… Mexes, and among my best employees."

It is obvious he holds these people in high esteem and I feel perplexed at why I had insinuated anything derogatory about the Mexican people. I have not had direct dealings with them, except for a short stint in the Tijuana jail while in the Navy. How do I correct my apparent anti Mexican stance I do not want to project. "They are doing great work for me!" I state as enthusiastically as I can.

He nods as he looks toward the roof and the patterns being formed by the workers slapping on shingles. "I... ah... had not noticed a problem with your roof, what happened that caused you to replace it?"

"The shingles are darkened in several places indicating a rotting condition of the wood roofing underneath." I state with as much authority as I can muster. I have no idea what I am talking about.

He is silent for several moments before saying softly, "Darkened?" He glances to his left at the house next to mine, "Come here." He says. I follow. "This is my roof." pointing at the roof two houses south of mine. "You see several shingles 'darkened'. This is not uncommon in this area of Texas, caused by humidity and not necessarily an indication of a problem. These houses are not yet ten years old and not ready for new roofs. Your roof should last from fifteen to twenty years. I think you may have been scammed. How much are they charging you for the replacement?"

I don't know, but cannot tell this man that. "Oh, they gave me a great price." I state emphatically.

"Around seven to eight thousand?" he asks.

"Yeah, ballpark." This is not purposely evasive, I don't know. Excusing myself, I re-enter my house. Searching my desk, I locate the copy I vaguely recall signing. Carefully opening the sheet I scan down the page until... "Holy shit! Sixteen thousand five hundred and seventy three dollars! Son-of-a-bitch!"

"There you are you dear man you!" She throws her arms around my shoulders as I am seated at the bar, giving me a wet kiss on the cheek. My surprise could not have escaped her but she appears not to notice as she takes the seat next to mine. Motioning to the bartender, she lights a cigarette before turning to me again. "I am just overjoyed that you are giving me your car, well, selling it to me for a dollar." She winks at me.

What the hell is she talking about? Give her my car? Who is this lady? She is probably sixty years old with grey hair, overweight with sagging jowls. Do I know her? "Do I know you?"

She spins toward me, her mouth open slightly, "Rick! After all we have been to each other these past few weeks? Do you know me? Don't tell me you have forgotten? You haven't forgotten the troubles I was telling you about with my vehicle and how you said you needed a new car anyway so you would give me yours? Surely you remember that." She smiles brightly at me.

"How ya doin' Helen, Rick? Good to see you two again." The bartender sets a glass of wine in front of 'Helen' and a Coors light in front of me. She knows what we drink. "Wow Rick! You're really something to give Helen a car. She has been so much in need of a dependable vehicle, you are really something! You're a great guy!" The bartender fondly expresses as she pats my hand.

Damn! I said I would give her my car? I would give her my car? I am an honorable man and if I said I would do something, then I am obligated to do it, but I don't remember this woman. I don't remember giving her my car. I have always been attracted to great beauty and cannot imagine why I would become involved with... this one. She is not ugly, but definitely not the beauty that is possessed by... well, the dark haired beauty alone at the end of the bar.

She looks more familiar than this grey haired old lady. Looking past the older woman that continues to talk without my hearing her, I study the woman sipping on a glass of red wine. She turns slightly away from us, but occasionally glances our way in the mirror. I would rather meet that one than this one whose prattle interrupts my thoughts.

"... and all you have to do is sign over the title... you did bring the title didn't you? You said you would last night."

"Last night?" I could not hide my surprise. Surely I would remember last night.

"Yes, you dear and you were incredible." She whispers leaning provocatively against me, her ample breasts pressing on my arm.

"Hummmph!" I grunt; I was incredible? I must have... we must have... she... damn!

"So, you did bring the title, didn't you?" She asks demurely as her left hand began to lightly rub the inside of my right leg, slowly moving up and down getting ever closer with each move until she was rubbing on my... oh my! She stands and places her left arm around my shoulders while her right hand takes the place of her left and gently massages me as she kisses my cheek and moans; "Let's go back to your place and consummate the title transfer on your bed?"

We undress quickly and I am put off by the sight of her overweight body, the pot belly, folds of flesh that hang over her hips, the very pale white breasts with blue blood vessels nearly covering the entire breast. Those breasts look like road maps and hang loosely against her stomach. I cannot get excited.

"Let me help you." She says as we lie naked on the bed. She gently took me in her hand and began to manipulate my manhood. I feel some heat rising in me, but know it is not enough to sustain a sexual encounter. Moving to straddle me, her large breasts brush against my chest. She kisses my neck, my chest and tugs on my chest hairs with her teeth. She draws in my nipples with her mouth and her lips continue to explore lower on my body until she... she... she... Oh God!

"So, Rick? What about that title?" She exhales the smoke from her freshly lit cigarette.

Re-entering the bar she gives a thumbs up signal to the couple at the end of the bar, a dark haired woman and a man that seems familiar... whoa! That's the man that did my roof! And that is... I suddenly remembered her name, yes that is Helen! "Helen?" I exclaim. Startled, she and the man quickly rise and leave the bar. "Was that...? I thought you said your name was Helen? What is going on here? Where is that title?"

The grey haired 'Helen' rushes out before I can stop her.

Confused, I look toward the bar. Was that Helen and the man that overcharged me for doing my roof, together? What do they have to do with the older 'Helen' that I gave my car to? Oh shit! I hadn't thought of this... not only do I not have a car, but how am I going to get home?

"Dad? You bought a new car?" Dawn asks in surprise.

"Yes, I needed a new one anyway."

"Why? You had less than thirty thousand miles on that car, why would you need to change?"

"There was almost thirty three thousand on it and... and... it was starting to give me some trouble..."

"Like what?" She angrily interrupts me.

"Well, there was a noise..." I find it difficult to explain and surely do not want to let my daughter know I gave my car away.

"What kind of noise? Was it a noise that could have been repaired? Dad, your car was only five years old. How much did you pay for this new one?" She is looking angrily at me.

"Thirty-four something.?"

"Thirty-four... thirty-four something!" Her voice trails off as she meanders around my kitchen absentmindedly touching items on my counter as she contemplates what to say. "Dad." She begins softly, "I know you can afford a new car; that is not the point. The point is you need to be more careful with your money. There are people who will take advantage of you. Your neighbor, D.J. told me about you getting a new roof. How much did you pay for that?"

"Ah, it wasn't much." I lie.

"How much." She is angry again. "How much?"

"Well if you must know, it is none of your business!" I shout back.

"How much Dad?" She asks softly.

I stare at her, neither of us flinch or take our eyes off the other. Finally she looked away and began to walk slowly toward the front door. I anticipated she would angrily slam the door as she left, but when the door does not open for several moments, I move to see what she is doing. She is in my office and has found it.

I try to grab it from her, but she puts the invoice behind her. We jostle momentarily as I try to retrieve the evidence of my stupidity. She bends away from me with the paper behind her. I will not physically fight my daughter and back away. She has a determined look as I try again to grab the invoice for my roofing deal, pulling it out of my reach. I sink into one of the chairs in front of my desk as she unfolds the invoice and begins to read down the page.

"Oh my God!" She looks at me. "Sixteen thousand five hundred dollars? What were you thinking?"

Chapter Eleven

People wave or return my greeting as I walk past their homes. Some are mowing lawns, or washing cars, others doing yard work, trimming around trees, bushes, or enjoying the sunshine. It is a beautiful day, sun shining brightly, a nice warm day for... what month is this? Doesn't matter, it is too nice to think about something that is not important. "Good afternoon!" I yell to a man washing his car. He hesitates, looks at his watch and replies. "Good morning to you sir." Did he say morning? Oh well, maybe I didn't hear him right.

The houses are all brick and different shapes, sizes and colors with mostly young couples engaged in caring for their homes. Large mature trees stand between the sidewalk and the street providing shade for the homes. The lawns are well manicured and I shake my head at the occasional home with excessive weeds choking out the grass. "Why can't he take care of his yard properly? Someone should knock on his door and tell him off." I laugh at the prospect of me actually going to a door and chastising the young man for letting his neighborhood go to pot. In a neighborhood as affluent as this, surely they can afford to have someone take care of the yard if they are too lazy to take care of it themselves.

At the end of the neighborhood, I reach a busy street with two lanes of traffic meeting me at high speeds. With no sidewalk along this street, I carefully walk on the grass well to the left of the approaching cars. Passing a gas station and later a mall with several shops, restaurants and a grocery store, I take note of a multitude of cars in the parking lot. Must be a busy place.

A car honks as I pass the opening to the mall, oops, have to move a little faster. He races the engine and spins his tires as I clear the way... must be mad. To hell with him, he can race his engine or squeal his tires or whatever, I don't care. It is safer to walk in the neighborhoods where the cars pass by slower and I do not have to worry about getting run over.

This is a nice neighborhood also. Not as many people outside now though, it is getting warmer, almost hot. I notice how bright the blue sky is, not a cloud in sight. The sun is almost directly overhead so must be close to noon. I look at my left wrist, hmmm... no watch. Why don't I have my watch? What happened to my watch? I never go out without my watch, well, I guess I can't say never anymore. HA! The sun casts shadows nearly straight down from the trees lining the streets, yep it must be noon.

Two girls in their early teens walk toward me on the sidewalk. Why aren't they in school? They laugh and giggle as they approach and suddenly stop talking and cover their mouths stifling a laugh. As they pass one says. "Zip up." What? What did she say? Zip, what does that mean? I walk a few steps and stop, zip up?

Leaning forward I look down, "Oh God!" How long have I been walking around with my zipper down? As I tug my zipper up I look over my shoulder after the girls and... see... him.

He slips between houses on the other side of the street. The teenagers are a block away now. A cold shiver comes over me as I see him, the pointy nosed one. He had not been outside before, or I'd never seen him outside my house, is he after me?

Taking tentative steps, I move to a position where I can see between the houses on the other side. Suddenly two ten year old boys come running out from between the houses, one chasing the other with a squirt gun, both laughing heartily. Was it them I saw? The cold chill returns as I peer between the houses and catch a fleeting glance of 'him' going around the back of the house. It was not the boys.

I turn and run, but quickly tire and have to slow to a walk. Checking over my shoulder, he is not in sight. However; someone or something is looking at me as the hair on my neck rises. Walking quickly, several blocks go by as I frequently survey both sides of the street to catch a glimpse of 'my friend'. He's not there.

Is that a park at the end of the street? Looks like a stream or a creek running along the back edge of the park. The steep bank behind the stream rises to a higher elevation and is mostly weed covered. A steep weed covered bank hides most of what appears to be the roof of a commercial building. This looks like a good place to stop and rest.

A sparse growth of trees offers shade on the benches in the park. I am tired and sit on a shaded bench.

How long have I been walking, how far have I gone? The stream is still fifty yards from this bench. I am alone in the park and relax in the shade as the warmth of the day engulfs me. This is peaceful. Birds rustle the leaves of the trees as they depart only to return a few moments later. Sunlight streaming through the leaves creates a mottled design on the ground, the design shimmering as the leaves stir in the light breeze. A squirrel climbs down the tree, circles the trunk upside down stopping to look at me. "Boo!" I say softly, he does not acknowledge me, but his tail twitches as he looks at me. I smile. He continues downward, then suddenly reverses direction and bounds quickly up the tree. Two young boys on bicycles ride by about thirty yards from my bench. The squirrel must have heard them coming. He is gone now, so are they.

An occasional car passes, intent on its own destination. I pay no heed. The warmth makes me sleepy. It is so peaceful here.

A noise awakens me and a group of young men, or boys… yeah teenagers, enters the park throwing a football around. About seven, no, eight boys in the group, some running out for passes as others organize a game. Other people occupy benches in the park, a mother scolds her child over some offense before sending him to play with the other children. How long have I been here? The shade from the trees has lengthened considerably. I look at my wrist, damn… no watch.

There is kickoff! The boys are divided into teams of four and chase or block for the one that caught the ball.

They stop, huddle up and shortly break into a run again as the ball is passed… ooh, incomplete.

Their shouts wake me, but I doze off again. Finally I awaken to silence, the football game has ended and the boys are gone. Only a few people remain in the park, wait… who is that behind those two women and the child on the bench, is that…? The cold chill returns as I recognize… yes, the pointy nosed son-of-a-bitch that I see with Kay. He is barely perceptible as he fades in and out behind the two women, like smoke. Fear envelops me as I stare at him. Is he looking at me? I can't tell for sure, wait… he is not there anymore, oh wait! There he is!

"Get away from me!" I scream. The two women on the bench stare at me. "Not you, him." I yell motioning at pointy nose. They look at each other and quickly pick up their belongings from the bench and start to push their strollers away. "No! No! You don't have to leave. It's him. He needs to leave me alone." They hurry away.

He is gone too, for when I return my gaze from the two young mothers, he is not in sight. Slowly I approached the bench the women were seated on. Carefully I walk around the bush behind the bench, ready to run if he comes at me. Completing the circular path, I stop and scratch my head. How did he get away so quickly? Returning to my bench I sit quietly.

The shadows have lengthened greatly and I am hungry, did I imagine seeing pointy nose? The women are gone and I no longer see… him. What time is it? Damn… no watch. Walking into the open area, the sun is near the horizon and will soon be dark. Stopping behind a tree, I peek around it to see if he is on the bench, yes... wait, no... oh damn, I can't tell for sure. One minute it looks like he is there and the next I see nothing. Is he playing tricks on me? Is he following me?

Leaving the park and crossing the bridge over the stream, the sun is touching the horizon as cars whiz past me. A last glance toward the benches in the park does not detect my 'buddy'. Where did he go? Got to get off this street, too many cars, I might get run over. Turning into the commercial area near the park, I seek a place to eat. Aw shucks, it's just a tire store, nothing to eat in here.

It is dusk and farther down the street I make out lights of other establishments, perhaps some place I can find food. A few minutes later I am disappointed to be walking past a gas station. Surely there is a restaurant nearby. What time... God damn it! More lights ahead, food? Finally, a McDonalds, I don't particularly care for their food but I am hungry so... enjoy.

A hamburger, fries and a soda fill me up. What was it we called a soda in Minnesota? Pop, yeah, we always called it 'pop'. Never drank anything stronger than pop, but then pop was quite a drinking man. That joke is still funny. I laugh.

Families with young children occupy most of the tables and booths and the mothers take charge of the children. The fathers that are here, mostly watch the mother tuck bibs, wipe mouths, feed or scold misbehaving kids. One notable exception is a father that roughly sets his not very unruly son into his chair and loudly scolds him. The boy was not being very bad. What had he done to anger the father so? "You want to cry?" The father yells, "You wait 'til we get home, I'll give you something to cry about!" Sheesh, he has... a mad... a mad... an anger problem. Poor kid, I wonder what he will grow up like. Like father like son? I hope not.

I think about the boy as I begin my return home. I recall occasions when my father yelled at me, but realized long ago that I deserved it, although at the time I felt he was wrong. Amazing how differently we see our parents later in life. Dad has been gone for what, ten years? Yeah probably, no wait, eleven years in September, mom is still going strong though. Golly, mom will be ninety-one in May, or is she ninety-one? Oh well, she still is fit as a fiddle as they say, still lives in the same house we lived in when I was a child. I cannot recall living anywhere else growing up.

A dog barks and rouses me from a trance-like walk. Where am I? This is a residential area and I no longer see the lights of the restaurant I ate at, what was the name of that place? Did I have something to eat? Well, I am not hungry so... yes, I must have had something to eat.

A sense of foreboding comes over me as I peer intently behind me. Is someone following me? The hair on my neck stands up as I feel a set of eyes on me. Fear envelops me, is 'he' following me? I cross the street for a different vantage point. Still do not,... wait... what was that? Did someone or something duck behind that tree? The branches are moving slightly.

I look around for a stick or something to use for a weapon? Seeing none I pick up my pace turning frequently to see if I am being followed. At times I do see something that disappears when it comes into the light of the street lamps. I am being followed. What direction am I going? Where am I going? Behind that bush... look there... what was that? Oh God! Are they after me? He is after me?

Street lamps light up the block and most of the homes have muted lights visible through curtains. None of the homes are familiar to me. My breath comes rapidly. Shall I go to a door and ask for shelter from my pursuer? No, I must get back to the safety of my house. Where is my house? I look at the street sign at the end of the block and do not recognize the name. Oh God, don't panic! Where am I? OK, OK, calm down, breathe, I am at the end of a block. Which direction should I go? Did I come from that way? What direction is that? Maybe it is best I go back the way I came. Which way is that? Is it that way? Wait, I didn't cross the street, or did I? Damn, a car is coming, gotta get out of the middle of the street. OOF, I trip over the curb striking my chin on the sidewalk. Ouch! God damn... that hurts! Little pebbles penetrate the skin on my right palm as well as my chin.

Rolling onto my back, I lay there to collect myself for a moment. It is a struggle to sit upright and finally I roll on to my knees and push myself up that way. Damn, I'm dizzy, it never used to be so hard to stand up. Someone is watching me. Shit! Is it him? Gotta run!

Tires squeal as a car careens to a stop before striking me. "Get out of the street you damned idiot!" the driver yells. Shoot, gotta watch where I am going. THERE HE IS! IN THE SHADOWS! HE IS LAUGHING AT ME!

"Laugh you son-of-a-bitch!" He chases me into traffic. I trip in fear over the curb again. "Help, oh somebody please help me." I whimper. Gathering my strength I scream, "HELP ME!" as loud as I can and roll myself into a little ball, grasping my knees and burying my face in them.

He grabs me by the shoulder as I cover my face and scream; "HELP! AAH! AAAAAH! HELP ME!"

"You alright buddy?" He says shaking my shoulder gently, real concern on his face. The driver stopped and reached out to me.

Oh thank God. "They're after me." I grab his arm. "Help me get away."

He looks around. "Who's after you?" He looks up and down the streets before returning his concerned gaze to me.

"Them... the ghosts... the pointy nosed one!" I frantically replied.

"Who?" He looks again down the street where I am pointing.

"They're behind the bushes, behind the trees, he's..." The man looks at me strangely. "Don't you see...? Can't you...?" I plead with him.

Gladly I enter his car as he opens the door for me, anything to get away from them. Covering my face with my hands I lie down on his back seat. He whispers into a cell phone and soon a patrol car appears on the scene. While one officer takes the drivers' statement, another asks for my identification and questions me about my name, address and what I am doing out this time of night. Soon the driver of the car that nearly hit me is waving goodbye and thanking the officers for coming.

"We'll take you home sir."

"Do you see them?" I crane my neck to see where my 'buddies' must be. "Is he still there?" Just as I thought, when someone comes that can take him into custody, he takes off for parts unknown. The son-of-a-bitch!

Chapter Twelve

Cars whizz past me on the left and the speedometer tells me I am driving at fifty miles per hour. This is not like me, I am not a fast driver, but normally drive the speed limit. What is the speed limit here, better yet… where is here? The traffic is not heavy, wherever I am. There are billboards, trees, and fields along the highway, none of which is familiar. None of it looks like… like… looks like what? Where the hell am I? That billboard says something about a motel in Joplin. Joplin? What the hell is a Joplin? It must be a place and does sound vaguely familiar, but how did I get here? How long have I been driving?

A flashing yellow light on the dashboard tells me I am almost out of gas. There is a billboard for a Flying J truck stop, I'll stop there for gas, and find out where I am.

"That will be thirty five ninety four, sir." the attendant drones as he waits. Reaching into my pocket I am surprised to find a large wad of bills, peel off three twenties and hand them to the attendant. Wow! Where did I get that much money? I hastily push the remainder back in my pocket and turn away.

"Sir! Your change!" The attendant yells after me.

"Thank you." I respond meekly, stuffing the bills and coins in my pocket.

The clank of dishes greet me as I enter the diner, a large woman hustles past me with a tray full of dirty dishes perched precariously above her shoulder. There are booths along the wall, sunlight streaming through the windows above them. In the center of the diner are six small tables for four people each, only two of which are occupied. A counter with several stools fronts the kitchen and the window that food is passed through. I found a seat at the counter. A large digital clock above the food window indicates it is three thirteen, I assume in the afternoon as the sun is shining.

"Can I help you?" The middle aged waitress asks. How do I respond? I say nothing. "Coffee?" She asks. I nod.

"What'll it be?" The waitress asks as she returns with a cup, pours my coffee and awaits my response. Perhaps it is the look in my eye as I stare at her, or my failure to respond, but she asks, "Are you OK?"

What is the answer to that? Am I OK? I don't know if I am OK. "I... ah... I ah... I don't know." I murmur softly.

Her eyebrows lift and she snorts as she pulls a stubby pencil from her hair and a notepad from her apron pocket, "You don't know if you're OK?"

Slowly I shake my head, "I don't know where I am."

"You're in the great state of Missourah, or Misery as some people put it." She laughs, tapping the pencil on the counter, "Joplin, Missourah to be more precise." Her laughter stops abruptly as she looks at me. Moving closer to the counters edge, she leans forward, a perplexed look on her face, and asks softly. "Sir? Are you OK?"

"I... ah... I ah... don't... know... can't remember... who I am."

Her brow furls as she asks, "You can't remember who you are?" She stands bolt upright, steps back with a stunned look on her face and calls out. "Al!" A man neatly dressed in tan slacks and a light blue polo shirt, turns from the table where he was sharing a laugh with a customer. The waitress whispers in his ear and he looks at me, then at her. "What did you say?" He exclaims and she whispers to him again.

The police officer gently holds my arm as he guides me into the Holiday Inn. Seating me in one of the lobby chairs, the officer approaches the clerk, speaking quietly.

Television programming doesn't appeal to me. It's all the same, every program a variation of another, or so it seems. I've had enough of this. I slide my legs over the side of the bed and slip my feet into my shoes. Not bothering to tie them, I open the door to see a young man who looks like an Ay rab, or someone from that part of the world, seated in a chair against the wall opposite my room.

He jumps up from his chair with a startled look, his books and papers spilling onto the hallway floor. "Sir, where are you going?" Well at least he speaks perfect English, no hint of an accent, maybe he isn't an Ay rab after all. Maybe he is just an American with a darker complexion. Now what did he ask me?

"What? Who are you?" I ask.

"Sir, you are not supposed to leave your room. They have asked me to see that you stay in your room and call the police if you try to leave, so please sir, go back to your room." He speaks as if frightened by something.

"The police? Am I under arrest?" I ask angrily.

"I don't know sir, I am just here to watch your room, and make sure you do not try to leave before your daughter got here."

"My daughter? My daughter's coming?"

"Yes sir, she should be here in a few... very soon." He bent down to retrieve his books and papers from the carpeted hallway.

I grunt, "My daughter." And turn partly away from him. My mind races wildly as I try to come up with a name, a face or anything. "What is her name?" I ask.

"My name is Khalid sir." He replies as he straightens out some papers.

I shake my head without saying, 'I don't give a shit about your name Ay rab, I want the name of my daughter'. It starts with a D... Dawn! That's it! Dawn! Damn, that was hard. Stopping in the doorway, I turn, "My daughter is coming here? Why don't I just go to her? You call her and tell her I am on my way. That will save a lot of time."

"Sorry sir. I was told you are to wait here. Dallas is six to seven hours away and your daughter was called over five... a long time ago and should be here soon." Khalid said softly.

"Oh." Wait! What did he say? Dallas? Six or seven hours? "Where am I?"

"You are in Joplin, Missouri sir."

"Joplin, Missouri? Where the hell is that? What the hell am I doing there?"

He shrugs. "Please sir. Return to your room. I just do as I am told."

The television drones on with repeating news stories and I begin to get a clearer picture in my mind of who Dawn, Jeff and Chad are. And where is Kay? How come she is not here with me? Will she be coming with Dawn? I know Dallas, or more precisely my home in Plano, but why had I come up here? Dale… Dale Lundy. He lives in Kansas City, he's always asking me to come up to visit him. Maybe I was… Joplin is on the way to Kansas City, maybe I was… oh damn, I don't know! How long has it been since the Ay rab told me Dawn was coming? Must be more than three or four hours, it's been a long time… I think.

A knock on the door connecting this room to the next arouses me from the program I am dozing through. Why is someone knocking on that door? Has <u>he</u> followed me?

"Who's there?" I ask cautiously, leaning close to the door.

"It's Dawn daddy."

"Dawn?" I freeze for a moment. Dawn? Oh yeah, it's not him, and open the door. "What are you doing here?" I ask and feel foolish as the answer probably has something to do with me.

"No! The question is what you are doing here." She exclaims sternly as she steps into my room. Behind her, Jeff glances shyly at me before looking away, trying to be nonchalant. "It's almost one O'clock in the morning, I am tired. What are you doing here? Why did you drive up here?" She's mad.

How do I answer that? I barely recall driving and am not sure why I came up here, or how I got here. Her eyes are flashing, cheeks reddened and she is mad, but I do not like being talked down to. "I came up here because... I wanted to." I reply defiantly.

"You wanted to!" She stares at me intently for a moment, "You wanted to... why? For what?"

There are moments when you have no answer and stand dumbfounded with nothing to say? This is one of those moments. I look at her, at Jeff, around the room, my hands and open my mouth to give a reasonable reply, but... "I don't know." I manage meekly. Dawn softens and grasps me in a warm embrace as I begin to cry. "I don't know."

The return trip to Plano the next morning is quiet. There isn't much to talk about. Jeff follows in my car, having slept in my room last night, and Dawn is in no mood to talk. Occasionally she says. "I don't understand what you were thinking." That made two of us.

"Oh there you are." I smile as she lay beside me. I did not see her get into bed, but she's been like that lately, kind of sneaking around. "I'm glad you didn't bring your friends today. That's alright, you don't need to say anything, I know you don't like to talk." Kay being here with me is comforting, it's like I go to another world and not bothered by anyone or anything.

"Mrs. Scott." The doctor greets Dawn before turning his attention to me. "Mr. Hageman. You have a form of Dementia, Alzheimer's, and in its early stages or phase one. We can prescribe some medication that may slow down the onset of the condition, but will not reverse it."

The word Alzheimer's struck me loud and clear but their conversational tone seems muted as if the doctor and Dawn step away to talk about me. Curiously, they are sitting near me and do not seem to have difficulty hearing each other but they are small and their voices come from far off, not a whisper, a very quiet tone as with the volume turned down. My breathing, as if in a barrel, echoes inside my head. The doctor and Dawn talk for some time, occasionally addressing me. I nod in response, but do not comprehend what they are saying. Wait, Alzheimer's? Holy shit! Isn't that what old people get? I'm not old, well OK, I am sixty-five but that is too young to have... that.

"I've just been forgetful." I state softly.

The doctor and Dawn stop their conversation mid-sentence and stare at me for a moment. The doctor is turned sideways holding a booklet toward Dawn. He closes the booklet and slowly leans back in his chair.

"Yes sir." He swivels his chair toward me and leans forward. "That is how it starts; one forgets things he

135

normally would not. Periods of memory loss, of recent events, become longer in duration. You can't remember what day it is, what month it is, or where you were going and why. It is a progressive disease and will get worse, I am sorry to say. We hope the medication will slow the onset to the point you will be able to function for quite some time, but... there will come a time when you will have to seek assistance." Picking up a brochure, he glances at Dawn before continuing with me. "I was just explaining to your daughter about The Good Samaritan Center and the many varied programs they offer..."

"Good Samaritan!" I interrupt. "Are you talking about an old folks home?"

"That is one of the programs, but we also have, what I am suggesting for you, an assisted living center where you will primarily be on your own with someone to 'assist' you, to check on you, should you need anything."

"I am not going to any God damned old folks home!" I defiantly stare at him and Dawn. Are they trying to put me away? I have a home where Kay can find me whenever she wants, will she find me in some other place?

"Daddy, it's what is best for you. Your house is just too big for you to take care of by yourself any more and..."

"And I like it there." I interrupt. "No thank you, I will stay in my house if it's all the same to you."

Dawn and the doctor exchange silent glances before the doctor leans forward to speak. Dawn holds up her hand and speaks in his stead.

"Daddy;" She begins softly, "You no longer have an option to stay on your own. With the police report... and your going off to Joplin... and the onset of... of this disease... you must have assistance that I cannot give. I cannot be with you to ensure your safety as well as see to your needs."

"I can be safe in my own home!" I angrily interrupt.

Dawn hangs her head. "Daddy." She pauses to collect herself. "At The Good Samaritan Center, they have a staff that will look in on you if you need anything. You will have your own room, your own T.V. your own furniture, a kitchenette, all the comforts of home... without... being at home. Daddy, your option is not whether to go into assisted living, but... to which assisted living center."

Damn! I try to form an argument but the words will not come and I am having difficulty figuring out what we were talking about.

Chapter Thirteen

What is this? This place is not familiar to me! This is a bedroom, I am lying in a bed, there's my clothes on the floor, but the room is much smaller than I remember. The bed is smaller too. I could not touch both sides of the bed at the same time before. Before... before what? Damn, that is perplexing, before what, before now? The room is a lot smaller too, what the... how can my bedroom shrink? And why is my bathroom not to my right as I roll out of bed? This is confusing. Where is my bathroom?

There are two doors on the wall to my left, both partly opened inward, darkness hiding the contents behind the doors. Another door, fully opened against the wall, reveals a room the contents of which are dimly lit.

Cautiously I stand beside the bed, 'Damn, I gotta pee!' and hurry toward a door hoping to find the bathroom. Success on the first try! As I sit there relieving myself, I look at the tiny bathroom and wonder why it is not the same as always. Has my bathtub always been in front of my toilet? The wash basin on my right also seems out of place. Damn! I can reach out and touch the bathtub.

I get a vision of four basins beneath a large mirror extending from the wall on the left all the way to the wall on the right. In front of the basins, a bathtub is connected to a large glass enclosed shower just inside the door coming from my bedroom. MY BEDROOM! Not this bedroom, this is not my bedroom! Where the hell am I?

"WHAT'S GOING ON! WHERE THE FUCK AM I?" I yell at the top of my lungs. I walk into the dimly lit front room, a davenport against a wall in front of me and a door to its left, a window on the wall to my right with the drapes pulled to minimize the sunlight. In a corner to the right of the window is a television set, but not **my** television. My television is much larger than this one. "WHERE IS MY TELEVISION?" I place my hands on my hips and scream, "SOMEONE STOLE MY TELEVISION!" anger building within me.

"Mr. Rick?" A soft voice is followed by a gentle knock on the door. "Mr. Rick? Are you OK?"

"Who's there?" I demand loudly.

"It's Irene sir." The muted voice comes from behind the door. "I heard you... um... well, stirring around and thought I'd see if you need anything. Can I come in?"

I reach for the door, but realizing I am undressed say, "Just a minute. I must put some clothes on."

A soft giggle, "Yes sir. That would be a good idea."

Picking up a pair of slacks off the floor in front of my bed, I hastily slip them on. "Who did you say you were?" I ask as I open the door.

"Irene." A stout young woman responds with a smile. "Is everything alright? I thought I heard a commotion a little bit ago. Are you OK?"

"Yeah! Well no, I mean... someone has taken my television and replaced it with this smaller set. What has happened to my big T.V.?"

"Mr. Rick; that is your television, your daughter brought it here from your home so you would be more

139

comfortable. Your big screen television is too large for this room and your daughter felt this one would suffice. It is a pretty big screen itself, thirty-two inches I believe, no one else here has a television that big."

"No one else has... wait a minute. What do you mean, no one else... here? Where is here?"

"This is The Good Samaritan Center for Assisted Living. We have other guests; they are the other ones I referred to."

"I'm in an old folks home?" I try to peer around her down the hall. I do not see or hear anyone down the dimly lit hallway.

"Oh no sir." She laughs, a big smile gracing her puffy cheeks. "This is an assisted care living center and, well, we do have people here you may classify as elderly, but our guests live without much help from us, just as you can sir. We are here to 'assist' you if you need anything from time to time."

I study her for a moment in her blue colored nurse's outfit, a notepad peeking out of a pocket on her ample hips.

"So, if I need anything you will come to help me? What is your name?"

"Irene sir, and yes. If you need anything from six PM to six AM, I will be the one to respond."

"So, it's..." I look at my wrist for my watch.

"Almost six AM." She finishes for me. "And the day nurse should be here any moment. I'll introduce you to her."

"How... how long... when did I get..." I stammer.

140

"When did you get here?" Damn, she is good at finishing my sentence for me. "Yesterday I believe, but I am off weekends and the guest list has you registered as a new arrival yesterday."

"Yesterday." You would think I would remember moving into a place like this.

A few minutes later, Irene knocks on my door again. I have been leaning against the wall behind the door and pull it open.

"This is Donna, Mr. Rick. She is your day nurse and will help you in any way she can."

"Good morning Mr. Rick. My you are an early riser. Out to get the worm are you, you early bird?" She laughs.

"I don't want a worm." Why would she think that?

"Just an expression." She says, shaking her head slightly. She is much taller than Irene, but then Irene is barely over five feet tall and Donna is perhaps five foot six or seven, perhaps medium height. She is also older than Irene by ten or more years although still a young woman. They must put the youngest ones on the night shift and let the older ones work the better hours. Donna is blond and weighs probably one hundred thirty to one hundred forty pounds, much less than Irene, and is pretty, I guess. Not pretty like Kay, but pretty enough I suppose.

"Mr. Rick, breakfast begins at seven-thirty if you care to join us in the dining area. You can of course, prepare your own breakfast if you prefer, but I think your daughter said you would not have food in your pantry until sometime this afternoon. We would like to know as soon as possible to plan for the number of meals to prepare. Can we expect you for breakfast?"

"What do you have for breakfast?"

Her countenance brightens as she recites the menu items. "You have your choice between eggs, fried or scrambled, oatmeal, grits and toast, cold cereal, fresh fruits, or pancakes, so... can we count on you for breakfast and lunch today Mr. Rick?"

"Can I have cold cereal and fresh fruits?"

"Certainly. Would you like some coffee and juice?"

"Thank you, yes."

They're not fooling me; this is an old folks home. I am easily the youngest one here, all the others being ten to thirty years older than I although each one looks to be fairly vibrant and sprightly, some more sprightly than others; although I will not challenge any of them to a race. For some reason I don't walk fast anymore, can't seem to pick my feet up, just kind of drag them along as I walk. Dawn says I should stop shuffling, pick up my feet and walk normally. Easy for her to say.

"... think?"

The old woman is staring at me as if she expects me to say something to her, or did she just say something to me. "What?" I ask, startled by the sudden realization the other three people at the table are looking at me, forks poised in mid-air awaiting my response. "I'm sorry. I must have... must have... what was the question?"

"Mr. Rick, I was voicing my concerns over the future of healthcare in the United States and wondered about your opinion. Do you think we should continue the privatized health care programs or go to government sponsored care for everyone?"

Holy shit! Who wants to think that hard? What the hell are they talking about? They look at me for a response although one of my tablemates is raising another forkful of salad to his mouth. "I guess I prefer we continue the current system of health care." I finally offer.

"But then how can those of us on a fixed income afford the ever increasing premium payments?"

"Yeah, I guess you are right. Maybe we should have the government take over health care."

"So you are in favor of socialized medicine?" Another chimes in.

"Harummph." I grunt and dig into my food. The peas roll off my fork as I try to pick them up. Mixing them in with my mashed potatoes makes them look like green boulders in a glacier, but now they are easy to pick up. What is this shit about health care any way, I don't want to talk to these old people about health care. Socialized medicine… isn't that a dirty word? And where was I at the beginning of the conversation? I do not recall sitting down at this table and do not know who these people are, or when they started talking to me. What do they want from me? Leave me alone.

"Harummph!" I grunt.

There are times I find myself talking with someone or being someplace I cannot remember going to. Each time I'd 'come back' in the middle of a conversation, a dinner or Dawn taking my hand. She comes to visit nearly every night… Oh wow! How long have I been here? I can't remember when I came, but then I don't remember not being here. Shit!

At least I have Dawn; her visits break up the tedium of the day, even if it is only for a few minutes. She has her own life and tells me about how Jeff is doing in his lawn care business... quite well the way it sounds.

I strain to recall how I lose myself in time, or wherever I go, but cannot bring it into focus. Wait, there it is, that's it. Sometimes I just lose focus, I mean... things fade away, voices get softer, people shrink in size and get fuzzy around the edges and then... just fade away. I come back in the middle of conversations or with someone talking to me about... something. How long am I away at these times? I don't know. No one seems to be able to tell me, but then I don't ask either.

The sound on the television starts to go down and I must be dozing off as the picture also starts to dim... and lose... focus....

I study the door for several minutes, trying to decide whether or not I should and finally decide, yes I will. Rising from my chair, I open the door and look down the hallway toward the counter behind which is a board with numbers and letters written on it. Seeing no one, what appears to be an outside door is to my right, I move toward it. It is an outside door. Someone comes in as I approach the door and I slip into a courtyard and take in the fresh air with a deep breath. Two women, one older and one younger, are seated on a bench in the courtyard and barely glance my way as I appear. On the horizon, the sky is a faint pink as the sun is setting and it is getting darker, just a few stars visible. I'll go for a little walk and be back in a few minutes. A car slows to a stop allowing me to cross the street. He spins his tires as he speeds on his way. I do not make out what he yelled, or why he yelled at me, as he passed. My feet do not move very fast but keep moving for some time. There is a slight chill, damn; I should have brought a jacket. Crossing my arms gives me some warmth, but it is chilly. What time of year is it? I'm cold.

How long have I been walking? City lights illuminate the sky blocking out the stars on the near horizon. Stars are visible if I look straight up. Beautiful! OOH, that makes me dizzy. This must be a residential area as there are several trees along the sidewalk, although few lights are on in the houses. How late is it? Is everyone asleep? Where the hell am I? There… there is a park and a bench. I am tired and cold, I'll sit down for a while and figure out what to do next. In the distance are traffic noises and close by is the sound of birds or something in the trees. Crickets… yes, I hear crickets. I really am tired; maybe I can lie down on this bench and rest for a while. Cold!

"Sir? Are you Rick Hageman sir?" A gentle shaking and the sound of a concerned voice awakens me. I peer at the sun low in the horizon and an out of focus form silhouetted against it. It is a police officer with another officer slightly behind him.

"Cold." I shiver.

"John, you want to get the blanket out of the squad?" The second officer does not respond but turns and walks briskly toward the police car parked at the curb.

"Um... What did you say?" I press my palm against my forehead trying to eliminate the cobwebs.

"Sir, are you Mr. Rick Hageman? We have been alerted to be on the lookout for a man that fits your description. Have you been living at The Good Samaritan?"

The second officer returns and drapes a grey blanket around my shoulders.

Good Samaritan. Hageman. Oh... yes. Rick. "Rick... yes... I am Rick. You have been looking for me? Am I lost?" I do not recognize the surroundings. There is the police car parked a few yards away, and a car that slows to turn at the next street. "Where am I?"

The two officers exchange glances and the nearest says; "Well, we're glad we found you. You are about three miles from The Good Samaritan. They issued a warning last night around eight PM that you had wandered away from the home and..."

"I just went for a walk." I interrupt softly.

"Yes sir. We will notify the home that we are returning you so you do not have to walk all that way back." The second officer spoke into his hand held radio, then stepped forward and said to his partner. "I've called it in."

Several of the staff members meet me as the officers walk me into the Good Samaritan Center. My fat nurse is crying and the tall skinny one puts her arms around my shoulders to guide me back to my room.

"Oh Mr. Rick, you had us so worried. We are so glad you are alright." The skinny one... what the hell is her name, practically gushes over me. "You must tell your daughter how we searched for you all night and how concerned we are for your safety. We called Dawn and told her you had been found; she should be here very soon."

"Who?"

"Dawn, your daughter."

I nod. "Oh."

"It was just one of those things, you know, bad timing. Irene had apparently just gone to get some coffee when you left your room. Normally there is someone else to monitor the hallways but Beth was sick last night and was in the... well you know, the facilities, so unfortunately there was no one at the aid station at that particular time. A family member of one of our guests told us someone went through the door as he entered but he did not mention that for over thirty minutes and by that time... well. We rushed outside but you were nowhere in sight. Irene has been disciplined, she is truly sorry for her mistake and I can assure you this will never happen again."

What the hell is she babbling about? "Harumpph!"

"DADDY!" Dawn rushes up and grabs me in a big hug. "OH daddy, we were so worried about you. Thank God you are alright."

I look at her and the six attendants surrounding us and wonder aloud; "Why wouldn't I be alright, I just went for a walk, what's all the big fuss about?"

"You didn't get much sleep." The skinny nurse... what the hell is her name... said to Dawn. "Irene told me you didn't leave here until after one in the morning."

"I didn't get any sleep thanks to you people. Why can't you do your jobs as you are supposed to?" Dawn angrily scolds her. "You're supposed to 'care' for him, you call letting him wander out on his own, care?"

"Mrs. Scott, Irene feels..."

"Irene! Irene is the one responsible! It is her responsibility to watch him is it not? She is the one that could have let him get killed, so don't talk to me about how Irene feels."

"Mrs. Scott..."

"Just... just..." Dawn holds her hands up to stop any further conversation. "Just leave us alone. I will take Daddy back to his room and get him settled down." She takes me by the hand and leads me away from that assembly.

Our conversation is not pleasant; I don't remember much of it, except that Dawn is mad at me.

"OH MR. RICK! What did you do?" Donna points to the mess in the middle of the living room floor. Someone had taken a 'dump' on the floor and then urinated all over it.

148

I look at the mess on the floor then at the nurse who is staring angrily at me. "What! I didn't do that! You think that I did that? I did not do that!"

"OK Mr. Rick. Calm down now. We will clean it up but if you need help getting to the bathroom, someone will assist you if you will just ask."

"I didn't do that. That is not mine." I state vehemently.

Donna came near and sniffed behind me. "Take off your clothes Mr. Rick? I'll clean them up for you while you take a shower."

"Dad, why did you make that mess in your room?" Dawn asks with obvious dissatisfaction.

"I didn't do that!" I insist.

"Then who did?" She yells.

"They did." I respond softly.

"They, who?" She is angry.

"You know… the… the…"

"And don't tell me it was your ghosts. You left them in your house; you did **not** bring them here with you." She shouts. That's what she thinks, but I do not argue with her. The dirty bastards shit on the floor in my living room and are making sure I get blamed for it. Kay was not here when they did it, although I did not see them do it, but she would not be a part of such a mean plan. I'll ask Kay tonight to tell the others not to do that anymore.

What is that acrid smell? And why are my eyes burning? There is a haze in the room and I find it uncomfortable to open my eyes or breathe normally.

"OH MY GOD, MR. RICK! Are you alright? Ken! Shut off that oven! Open the windows! Get some fans in here to clear out the smoke." Donna shouts orders to the young man that goes quickly to my stove. Turning to me, she speaks softly, "Are you OK Mr. Rick?"

"What's going on? What happened? Who... what..."

She looks at me, a cross between disgust and concern on her face.

Ken opens the oven door to my stove and, grabbing pliers from his pouch, grasps the edge of a pan and disappears out the door to my room.

Donna turned back to me and began sternly. "Were you cooking something Mr. Rick?"

"No." I told her truthfully. "I was going to go to dinner with... with... well with my friends that I always have dinner with."

"You were not trying to cook something?"

"No, of course not. Why would I cook something if I was going to... why them bastards! They are doing it to me again."

Donna hangs her head, her blond curls hiding her face, "No Mr. Rick. They did not do this to you, you did this yourself and we cannot have you endangering yourself and the other guests here."

"But I did not do this. They want me to get into trouble... they want..."

"MR. RICK! STOP IT!"

She scared me, "Don't yell at me, I don't like it." I whimper.

She hung her head and said nothing, nor did she look at me. Ken returned, "It was a piece of meat, I think. Pretty well charred and burnt, probably been in there several hours on broil."

She picked up her head and looked at Ken for a moment. "What are the other guests doing?"

"Most of them are in the dining area and only recently noticed the smell of smoke. They have been kept calm and will be OK."

She was silent for a time. "Thank you Ken, will you see to the fans; and why didn't the smoke alarms go off?"

"Yes ma'am, I'll check on them." he asserted as he left.

She appears grief stricken as she states softly, "I must call your daughter."

Chapter Fourteen

"I know now that it was your mother."

"Dad!"

"It was! She came through the porthole in the closet and..."

"DAD! Stop it! It was not mother. It is not any one else, not ghosts not... not any one and most of all not mother. No one is trying to "get you" or make bad things happen to you! You are doing all this to yourself."

I am shaking my head before she can finish. "No! I swear. It was..."

"SHUT UP! I don't want to hear it any more. Just... stop... stop... stop it." She is crying, covering her ears with her hands. Why doesn't she believe me? I am not making this up.

She takes my hand as she wriggles forward in her chair. Mr. Nelson sits as an interested observer, slowly tapping his pen on his chin as he looks at us. I had not had an occasion to meet him until today when Dawn introduced him as the administrator of The Good Samaritan Assisted Living Center.

"Daddy." She begins quietly in a tone that tells me I will not like where this conversation is going. "Daddy, you can't stay here any longer."

"Whew! That's a relief! I thought you were going to tell me something bad. Great! Now I can go home and get out of this jail, I don't know why the police have me…"

"DADDY!" She shocks me with her loud tone.

"Mr. Rick, I…" The administrator began, but stopped abruptly as Dawn angrily held up her hand.

"You can get the idea of going back to your house out of your mind because that is not going to happen. You cannot be trusted to stay alone."

"But it…"

"I'm not finished!" She sternly cut me off. She looks at me and I see… well, pain, perhaps exasperation. "You have demonstrated you are a danger to yourself and others, and… DON'T SHAKE YOUR HEAD AT ME, JUST LISTEN!" Damn, is she ever mad!

She looks at the floor for several seconds before looking at Mr. Nelson, then at me. "You have proven to me, and to all, that you cannot take care of yourself and can no longer be given the freedom to live here at the assisted care center. Mr. Nelson has agreed…" She pauses, looking at him for support before continuing. "To move you into Memory Lane…" She pauses again as Mr. Nelson stops tapping with his pencil, his face changing from surprise to acceptance as he nods. "Mr. Nelson will see to it you have the care you require with your Alzheimer's that has progressed to stage four. You will not be allowed to leave the center without a responsible escort, which will not be very often, if at all. You will have your own room, but not the comforts you have had here. I will make it as comfortable as possible, but your freedom

153

will be restricted. You will be watched very closely as you are considered a flight risk."

"I don't know how to fly."

Mr. Nelson could not stifle the quick laugh, but quickly covered his mouth and turned slightly to the side.

"That's not funny dad." Dawn hangs her head.

I'm not trying to be funny, I can't fly. I can't fly an airplane either and did not intend to get a ticket for a flight to anywhere. So what is funny about that?

"Who are you? What are you doing here?"

"This is Mr. Rick, Dolly. He will be staying here with us." The young attendant tells the inquisitive old woman.

"No he won't. He's not going to stay here. I don't want him here." Her silver grey short hair is pulled back into a bun, secured by a rubber band. She is remarkably fit for one seventy-five or so years old. "And who is she?"

"This is Mr. Ricks' daughter, Dolly. Can you say hello to her?"

"Don't want to. She's going to steal everything, can't let her see in there. She'll steal everything, can't let her in."

"Dolly, this will be Mr. Ricks' room and his daughter is here to help get him settled in, don't you want to make them feel welcome?" He is a very pleasant young man of maybe twenty. He looks Middle Eastern... like an Ay rab.

"Are you an Ay rab?" I ask as Dawn clicks her tongue in horror.

He smiles gently, "My Grandparents came from India many years ago, so I'm Indian."

154

He doesn't look Indian. I look at him a moment then tap my mouth with my hand three times.

Dawn exclaims. "Dad!"

He laughs. "No… no… not that kind of Indian. We came from India, you know, where the Taj Mahal is, that kind of Indian."

The old grey haired woman looks at me and grabs my arm. "Where you from?"

"Dolly. You know not to touch anyone. Let go of his arm please." He is gentle but firm with his tone and Dolly let go immediately and walks away displaying a sprightly walk as she throws her hands up in the air and mutters something indiscernible.

"Mrs. Scott, my name is Steve and I will be the one primarily involved with your father. We will get along just great won't we Mr. Rick." He says turning his attention from Dawn to me.

"Yep." I smile and tap my fingers to my mouth.

"Daddy!" Dawn starts, shrugging her shoulders and smiling apologetically toward Steven.

"That's OK Mrs. Scott. It will be something between your father and I, won't it Mr. Rick?" This is a very likeable young man.

"What are you doing in here?" Dolly exclaims and is not far into my room before Steve swiftly moves in front of her to guide her out of my room.

"Dolly, this is Mr. Ricks' room, you need to let him have his privacy."

"He stole something from my room. I want it back."

"Dolly, Mr. Rick has not been in your room. He has not taken anything from you." Steve assures her as he gently leads her away.

"He came into my room last night."

"No Dolly. It's OK. Here's Rita. Do you want to talk with Rita?"

Rita looks up at the pair. "I have children. Lots of them, there's..." She pauses, looking bewildered. She too is about seventy-five, overweight and not as active as Dolly. Rita sits in a straight backed wooden rocker and only looks up when someone speaks her name. "There's... and..." She stops, her eyes darting back and forth. "I have children." She finally says softly.

It's so boring here. We listen to music on the radio or player or whatever is providing the music from my youth. A Gene Pitney song; "A Town Without Pity" is playing; he could be singing about this place. We sit here quietly, except Dolly of course, that bitch is up roaming around constantly yapping and getting into other peoples' business. She never shuts up, always nosy, asking stupid questions that have been answered a million times. I don't know how Steve maintains his demeanor with her.

I watch television occasionally but never did like daytime programming. Sometimes I turn on old movies but sleep through most of them. I also fall asleep in the day room when I go out there. Damn, I sleep a lot these days. Better if I get up and walk around a little, or shuffle, I don't move very fast anymore, and my feet have begun to swell around the ankles. Got fat ankles now, they don't hurt though.

"Where you going?"

Oh shut up Dolly. You're starting to piss me off.

"You going someplace? What are you going to do? I bet you're going someplace you shouldn't. You're going to take something aren't you?" She came right up to me.

"Shut the hell up!" I mutter softly as I ball up my fist and strike her in the face, knocking her to the floor. Steven breaks into a run; he had been walking toward us to keep Dolly from me, but is too late to prevent her from getting her due. Another attendant quickly comes to aid Dolly.

"Mr. Rick. Please stay here for a minute." Steven says softly as he moves me into my room before returning to check on Dolly.

"What happened? What happened?" Dolly asks the attendant helping her from the floor and gently wiping blood from her nose.

"It's OK, Dolly. You'll be OK. No serious damage. Ooh! Your eye is beginning to get red around the edges a little. Let me get some ice on it to keep the swelling down."

"What were you thinking?" Dawn is admonishing me again. I don't like that. She seems to be criticizing me out a lot lately.

"About what?"

"About what? About hitting Dolly Dad, what else would we be talking to you about. Mr. Nelson has been patient with you but if you cannot get along with the others in this unit..."

"She was in my face."

Dawn looks at me with surprise. "That is no excuse dad. You don't go around hitting people."

"She had it coming."

"No she didn't."

"She was bugging me."

Mr. Nelson spoke up. "I see no evidence of remorse, I see no recourse but to..."

"Mr. Nelson, please. I beg of you. He will get used to being here, it's all new to him. He will be a good citizen, he is a good citizen, just give him a chance, he'll get along with people. He has never been confrontational. This is an isolated incident, I'm sure he won't do it again. Please."

The fifty something man, with hair graying at the temples, ponders Dawns' plea for several moments, struggling to make a decision. He wears a grey suit with a maroon tie around the neck of his white shirt. The white shirt looks to be about two or three sizes too big as there is a large gap between the shirt and his neck. He fiddles with his hands in silence.

Finally he sighs and moves forward in his chair. "OK." He begins. "But this is his final warning. He will be classified as violent and as such the cost of his care will by necessity go up as he will have to be monitored more closely. Should there be a re-occurrence you will have to find some other place for him."

"I understand sir. Thank you, you will not be sorry, you'll see."

Steven is closer to me than he had been and another attendant also spends more time in the area. I'm not violent, I'm not mad at any one! Why does everyone yell at me?

Dawn says my brother Don is coming to see me. She showed me a picture of him, who the hell is that? He doesn't look like me at all. He's my brother?

"Hey Rick, how ya doin' buddy? You doing alright?" Don says as he greets me.

"Yeah." I reply. Now I know why he doesn't look like me, he has a mustache. I never had one of those. I reach toward the mustache but he flinches away from me.

"Whoa. Trying to get my nose are you." Don laughs. "You remember my son John don't you Rick?"

"Yes." I lie, staring at the young man at my brothers' side. He is the same height as my brother but does not have grey hair. His is a dark brown.

"John was recently married Rick. Maybe soon we can bring his wife down to meet you, would you like that?"

I shrug.

For a couple hours we engaged in small talk, me mostly listening and Don trying to find things to talk about and, - what was his name, the kid, - oh yeah John, entering into the conversation only briefly. I show them my room and they fawn over how comfy it seems. Yeah right! We go outside and sit in the sunshine for a long time while I doze off repeatedly. I am beginning to lose focus.

Rick has been asleep on the couch for a few minutes so I let him sleep. He is my big brother, someone I have always looked up to. He is the one the family could always count on in time of need. He has been my rock in my times of trouble, now here he lies, so dependent, so weak, so vulnerable. As I look up, I happen to catch Dollys' eye.

"Where you from?" She asks immediately.

"Minnesota." I reply casually.

"I know somebody from there." She states. "What are you doing here?

"I'm here to see my brother Rick."

Looking at John, she demands, "What are you doing here? You here to take all my stuff?"

John is taken aback. "Wha..."

Steven answers for him, "Dolly, no one is here to get your stuff. It's OK. You go talk with Rita."

"I have children." Rita starts as she looks up from her daze.

"I've got lots of children." Dolly counters walking toward the woman in the rocking chair.

The other three women living in this section, two of which are wheelchair bound, do not enter into conversations, just stare at the floor. They probably think it useless to talk with Dolly.

"I have five." Rita states softly, "There is... there is... and..." Her eyes dart back and forth as she tries to come up with names.

"I got lots more than that." Dolly counters proudly.

John asks Steven, "Does she?" Steven shrugs.

Steven stands and motions toward Dolly, "Dolly, would you like some ice cream?"

At the mention of ice cream, Rick pulls his head up and looks around. "Would you like some ice cream Mr. Rick?" Steven continues.

Dolly turns to me, "Where you from?"

"Minnesota." I state again as Steven retires to the kitchen and returns with two paper cups of ice cream complete with small wooden spoons I recall from my youth, hadn't seen those for a long time. I watch my brother struggle to lift the tab on the side of the cup and wonder if I should open it for him. A phone rings on the desk in the hall leading to the dining area, on the second ring Rick lifts his ice cream cup to his mouth and says, "Hello." John and I exchange glances, is my brother trying to be funny? No one laughs. I take the cup and open it for him.

"Where you from?" Dolly asks again.

"Minnesota." I repeat. This one is getting to be a pain.

"I know somebody from there. What are you doing here? Why'd you come?"

"I came to see my brother Rick."

Dolly looks at Rick sitting off kilter on the sofa next to me slowly lifting the ice cream into his mouth. "He sleeps a lot doesn't he?"

"I guess so." He does seem tired, the ice cream cup dangling from his hand lightly resting on his leg. I don't know what to say to him, I can't return to Minnesota

161

yet, our flight doesn't leave until the day after tomorrow. I hope John and I don't just sit here and watch Rick sleep. I take the ice cream, get up and walk toward Steven standing a few feet away. He positions himself between Rick and Dolly.

"Steven. Does he sleep like this every day?" I ask.

He ponders the question a moment. "Not every day. There are days when he does sleep for much of the day and others where he is awake and lively much of the time."

Almost as on cue, Rick opens his eyes and looks to the side at John. I return to his side and he stares at me. I try to engage him in conversation again, but as before, I do all the talking.

Rick is looking at my feet, or the carpet, and finally looks at me. "You have a dog on your feet?"

"What!" I laugh, "A dog on my feet?"

"Yes, be careful when you move so you don't hurt him, he's just sitting there quietly, he has been for some time now."

I sit up slowly pulling my legs in.

"Now you did it! He's gone." Rick whispers disappointed.

John looks at me, waiting for me to say something profound, I guess. I look at Steven, he must be used to this for he doesn't waver in his posture or change his expression.

"OK Rick. John and I are heading back up North again. It was good to see you, take care of yourself OK?" Don says as he and what's his name say goodbye.

"Is it a nice place up north?" I ask.

The two of them look at one another a moment before Don said. "Yes, very nice, cold this time of year though. We don't have it nearly as nice as you do here… weather wise." Don adds hastily.

It was quiet for a couple of days until Dawn came again to visit. She doesn't come every day any more, busy I guess.

"Did you enjoy Dons' visit dad? Too bad he doesn't live closer, you could see him a lot more often then." She said bending over to pick up my dirty clothes for the laundry.

"He's just upstairs." I counter.

"No, he and John went back to Minnesota."

"He's upstairs. He lives in the apartment upstairs." Why is she looking at me so strangely?

"Dad, there is no upstairs."

Steven steps into my room from his position by the door and says. "Would you like some ice cream Mr. Rick. Maybe I can show your daughter where it is so she can get it for you when she comes."

"I know where…" Dawn starts but stops as she looks at Steven and walks into the kitchen area with him.

Chapter Fifteen

"Dale Lundy here to see Rick Hageman please." I inform the woman at the front desk.

"Rick Hageman..., Rick Hageman." She mumbles as she looks through files on her computer. "Yes, here it is... Rick Hageman. He's in Memory Lane. Take the aisle to the right to the second aisle on your left, to the next aisle to the right, to the double doors, knock and someone will let you in. I'll call ahead and tell them you are coming." She says politely pointing down the aisle to our left.

We are very apprehensive about this visit. Rick and I have been like brothers since our High School days in Minnesota. We joined the Navy together, I was best man at two of his marriages (only missing the marriage from hell), and he had been best man at my wedding. I married his cousin and can thank him for introducing us after he and I got out of the Navy. Diane is also apprehensive as her father died a few years ago from complications brought on by Alzheimer's. Now her cousin, my best bud, my brother by other parents, as we stated so many times, is afflicted with this debilitating disease.

Dawn warned us this would not be a pretty sight, but I have to see my 'brother'. We left Kansas City, Missouri, early this morning and drove for nearly nine hours to get here. We plan to spend tonight and tomorrow and return home Sunday.

We are met at the double doors by a thin attractive young man that looks to be of Indian descent. "You're here to see Mr. Rick?"

"Yes, Rick Hageman."

"He's in room one-oh-one. Come, this way, I'll see if he is ready." Diane and I follow him past a large dimly lit room where two elderly ladies in wheelchairs stare at their hands. My heart is in my throat as we stop in front of a door with the numbers one, zero and one on it.

"Mister Rick. Are you decent?" The young man smiles at Diane as he asks this question.

"NO!" came a loud reply from within.

"Who are you? What are you doing here?" An elderly lady in her mid to late seventies with silver grey hair asks as she boldly strides up to me.

"Dolly. These are friends of Mr. Rick. They came to see him." The young man asserts quietly but firmly.

"Who's in there?" Dolly asks as she pushes on the door to Rick's room. The young man uses his left arm to block her entrance and closes the door with his right hand.

"Now Dolly, this is Mr. Ricks' room, we must respect his privacy remember?" He says gently.

"Who is it? Oh yeah. What are you doing here?" She says turning to Diane.

"I'm here to see Mr. Rick." Diane replies with a smile.

"No you're not. You're here to steal everything. Can't have it though, can't be taking my things." She says, turning away from the door. Suddenly she wheels about and tries to push past the young man. "Who's in there."

"Stay out!" Rick shouts from within.

"Dolly, please let Mr. Rick have his privacy." The young man says gently as he again blocks her attempted entry.

This young man has a lot of patience or perhaps has gained his patience with experience. Could not be much experience as he surely is not more than twenty years old. Dolly walks away mumbling incoherently. The three of us stand outside the door in uncomfortable silence for a few seconds. The remarkable young man continues to have a bright smile on his face the entire time.

"Are you getting dressed Mr. Rick?" He asks.

"Yes." Is the quiet reply.

"Maybe we should wait over there." My wife indicated the couches in the main room. We find a seat and are soon joined by Dolly on the next couch.

"Where you from?" She asks, poised on the edge of the couch.

"We're from Kansas City." I state.

"Oh. I know someone from there. Where you from?" She asks Diane.

"I'm from Kansas City too." Diane responds cheerily.

"Yeah. I know someone from there." She said.

"I have children." The elderly lady that has been rocking in the chair to our right says as she looks up at us.

"I've got more." Dolly says to no one in particular.

"I have five. Three boys and five girls. Their names are… are…" The rocking lady goes silent, eyes darting back and forth. "I have five boys." She quietly states, her voice trailing off before she stares again at her hands in her lap and resumes rocking. She rocks slowly, head cocked slightly to the side, hands clasped together in her lap, blank, sad eyes staring at a point on the floor not too distant but seeing who knows how far in the distance.

The young man stands sentinel by the door to my buddies' room, the first door to the right in the hallway adjacent to the large day room. A female attendant writes in a ledger at a desk between this large day room and what appears to be a kitchen and dining area. A small fluorescent light above her desk provides light for her to work by. The room is softly lit with much of the lighting provided by the afternoon sunshine filtered through thin white lacy curtains on westward facing windows.

I glance at my watch and note it is a little past three in the afternoon. Dawn agreed to meet us at the home around three, so she should be here soon. Finally after another five minutes pass, the young man standing near the door moves toward the door, an indication Rick is coming out.

My heart drops as I see, not the man six months my junior, but one appearing to be twenty years my senior. His thinning hair has greyed substantially and is not slicked back as neatly as always. His complexion is yellowed and he has lost some weight, probably twenty or so pounds.

Slowly he enters the hallway shuffling his feet along as the young attendant matches his stride, taking one step for every three or four that Rick does. Ricks' head is bowed staring at his feet as he barely shuffles along. He is but a few feet away from his door when I jump up to go to him.

"You have some guests Mr. Rick." The young man says.

Rick looks up and his face brightens. "Dale Lundy." He says with a smile.

"How ya doin buddy." I gush enthusiastically, taking his arm from the young man. Diane kisses Rick on the cheek as she takes his left arm to help him to the couch.

"You won't believe this." Rick begins softly as we move toward the couches. "But I know everything that is going on."

"I have no doubt." I say as I look over Rick's head into Diane's pained eyes. I start to ask what he has been doing, but already know that life in a home such as this does not offer much in the way of excitement. "So." I manage feebly, - great conversationalist. "It's good to see you Rick."

"Hmmm."

Apparently he is not much for talking either.

"What are you doing here?" At least Dolly can talk and obviously does so with little or no provocation.

"I'm here to see my buddy Rick." I say with as much enthusiasm as I can muster, grasping him around the shoulders and shaking him gently for Dolly to see.

She stares at us for a moment then asks, "Where you from?"

"Kansas City." I respond, not surprised by her repeated question. I know, or at least have been told, Alzheimer patients do not remember much on a short term basis. They apparently retain memories from years ago, but may not recall yesterday or more recent events.

"Where you from?" She directs at Diane.

"I'm from Kansas City too." Diane answers cheerily. "I've come to see Rick. Where are you from?"

Dolly ignores the question, or perhaps does not know the answer.

"I have five boys." The lady in the rocking chair states as she looks up from the attention she has been giving the floor in front of her.

"I have more." Replies Dolly.

Rick's head is bowed again and I lean over to see if his eyes are closed.

"What are you doing here?" Dolly is persistent if not obnoxious.

I look at her and smile. "I've come to see my best friend, my brother from other parents, right?" I say gently shaking Rick.

"Ummm." He barely nods, but I detect a slight smile.

Long term memory intact, is that true? "Do you remember when we hitch hiked from San Francisco, catching a military hop in Salt Lake City to Springfield Massachusetts on our way to Minnesota?" He smiles slightly. "How we fantasized about parachuting out over Minnesota so as not to go so far beyond? How we got drenched in the heavy rain along the tollway in New York and the one hundred mile per hour ride with the salesman and how nervous we were?" I pause to look for recognition, or a sign that tells me he remembers.

"Remember what happened in the Greyhound bus terminal in Chicago, the ten dollar bill you held in your hand?" He is smiling. "Yes, you remember the girl at the other counter accepting an offer you had not made as you held the ten dollar bill. How we only had two days at home before having to leave, again with our thumbs out, in twenty-five below zero weather?" I gently massage his shoulders. He is smiling, I think he does remember.

"What are you doing here?"

"Dolly." Diane responds for me. "We've come to see Mr. Rick."

"Where are you from?"

"Kansas City."

"I know someone from there."

"I have children." The woman in the rocking chair by the windows interjects.

Rick does not visibly respond to verbal stimulus.

The young attendant is seated on the couch near Dolly and Diane tries to mask her angst as she strikes up a conversation with him. "How long have you been working here?"

His eyes dart about and he sees we are focused on him. "About a year, I started just about this time last year."

"Wow! You seem to have a way with the... ah, with the patients. Is this what you want to do as a career?" Diane asks.

"No ma'am, I enjoy this, but I am going to school in hopes of becoming a lawyer."

"How old are you?" I have to ask as he seems so mature but looks so young. "Where are you going to school?"

"I am twenty two sir, a senior attending night classes at SMU so I can work here to pay for my schooling."

"What is your name?" Diane finally got around to asking what perhaps should have been asked first.

"My name is Steven."

"Steven? I would have thought you would have had..." I am getting myself into an embarrassing situation if I continue to follow the foreign looking path.

Steven smiles, "My grandparents came from India before my parents were born and the whole family is proud to be American, thus an American name was chosen for me."

He let me off the hook before I firmly wriggled on it.

"Wow Rick! Your feet are really swollen." I state returning my attention to our reason for being here.

"Yes." Steven interjects. "He should keep his feet up when he sits, but he likes to walk around a lot and his feet swell up like that."

I retrieve a straight backed chair, sit down facing him and put Ricks' feet on my lap, and massage them. "Does that feel better?" Is it the rubbing of his feet that makes his head bob up and down slightly or is he saying it does feel good. His head continues to move up and down unevenly as I silently massage his feet.

"Where you from?" Well…, so much for silence. I see why Rick popped this old bag.

"I'm from Kansas City, Dolly. I've come to see my best buddy, Mr. Rick. My wife is from Kansas City too. She also has come to see Mr. Rick. He is her cousin." I try not to sound exasperated but she is beginning to try my patience. I have a great appreciation for attendants, such as Steven, who are with patients like this day after day and are able to refrain from showing, or being, exasperated.

Dolly looks at us for a few seconds. "I know someone from there."

"I have five boys." I wonder if she will remember their names this time.

"Ummph" Rick grunted.

A female attendant wheels another patient into the room pushing her chair close to the arm of the sofa where I am seated. This patient is in her late eighties at least and stares at me. Her fingers waggle feebly trying to reach me.

Diane gets up and goes into the kitchen. I know this is getting to her as it is getting to me. She is more sensitive than I, although I feel a great lump in my throat and have fought back tears since our arrival. This is a man that in a year and a half since I last saw him has aged tremendously and is not the vibrant, in control personality he had been. He had always been at the forefront, offering assistance to anyone that needed it, now he is... dependent... unable to care for himself.

Wiping her eyes, Diane came back and asked softly. "Can we go?"

I shake my head. It is nearly four thirty and Dawn is not here yet. "I'm going to call Dawn and see if she was detained." I had to go to our van to get her cell phone number. Diane came with me.

"I'm almost there." Dawn says into the phone, "I thought we were going to meet at Dad's house and had been waiting for over an hour for you."

"I'm sorry. I thought we agreed to meet at the home."

"Yeah, dad's home. Wait, did you mean the home where he is now? Oh well, I'm only a few blocks away now and will be there shortly." Dawn said cheerily. We have known Dawn for all her life having waited in the hospital with Rick when she was born.

Dawn pulls up next to our van and slides out the drivers' side of her SUV. She smiles as I give her a hug. "Shocking isn't it?" She says in a matter of fact tone as she gives Diane a hug before returning her gaze to me.

"Yeah." I breathe softly. "You told me it would be, but..."

"I know. It's hard to prepare yourself for that."

"I tried." I shrug my shoulders. I lightly rub Diane's back, gaze skyward and try to continue, "I ah... I... damn!"

173

"I saw some of this with my dad when he had Alzheimers, but Rick is too young..." Diane interjects, sensing my inability to speak.

Dawn nods. "That's what he said... Dad. Dad said 'I'm too young to have lost my mind'... tore me up."

"Yeah, he told me he knew everything that was going on."

"And he does... most days, but there are some days he does not have a clue as to what is going on, or where he is, or even who he is. Has he told you about Don living upstairs here?" I shake my head. "As you can see this is a single story facility. There is no upstairs, yet to dad, Don is living upstairs."

"It would be funny if it wasn't so sad." I say.

"Oh I laugh at it. If I didn't it would drive me crazy, so yeah, I laugh a lot." Dawn pauses a moment. "Has he told you he is in jail?"

"No."

"Well that's good. He feels he is being persecuted by the police and has been put in jail. We try... well I hope we have him convinced he is in a hotel and not jail."

"He thinks he's in jail?"

Dawn nods. We stand there a while, none of us having much to say before Dawn breaks the silence. "Ready to go back in?"

"Yeah, we can only stay a little while longer, then we have to go." I say sneaking a glance at Diane.

"I understand, it's not easy."

Rick is on his side on the couch, eyes closed when we return. I sit on his left side, reach my arms around him and pull him upright. Dawn seats herself to his right and begins rubbing his shoulders. Rick opens his eyes, turns his face to her and smiles brightly, his love for her clearly evident.

"How are you dad?" Dawn asks the question probably asked each time she comes. He smiles. Dawn looks at me as she addresses her father. "Are you glad Dale came to see you?"

"No." He states softly, lovingly looking at Dawn.

As she peers at me solemnly over her father's head, "You didn't want him to see you like this did you."

"No."

Dawn knew what his answer would be, but his answer cut me deeply. I do understand as I may feel the same way if our roles were reversed. How can anyone understand? He is so helpless.

Diane looks at me, her face contorted and eyes reddening. "Can we go?"

I say nothing for a moment, afraid to admit how uncomfortable I feel in the presence of my best friend. I must overcome this feeling, must find something to say to make him feel better, must... "OK. Dawn, we have to get going." Damn I am weak! "Rick. I love you Rick. Brothers always? You take care of yourself, OK? I love you buddy. I'll try to come see you again soon, but in the meantime, you take care alright buddy?" I hate myself.

We do not stay the second day as planned.

Chapter Sixteen

OK. So I'm in a hallway, surely it isn't a very narrow room. How did I get here, and when did I get here. And it's a hallway of what, where?

"What are you doing?" Some old skinny, nosy broad inquires. Steven,... yeah, that is his name, the dark skinned Ay-rab, is beside me. Has he been there all the time? My steps are halting, moving in small jerks as I press my feet forward; they move such a short distance. I study them barely lifting off the floor, my feet moving but inches with each step.

A fog is creeping around the edge of my vision, darkness closing in on me. The wall wavers and tilts toward me as I lose my balance, fall against it and slump to the floor. Steven is not strong enough to keep me from falling but does soften the blow as I land on the thin brown carpet.

"Mr. Rick! Are you alright? Mr. Rick!" Steven shouts excitedly as he leans forward to help me, at the same time motioning, seeking assistance from another attendant. A nurse with a foreign accent rushes to help, taking my right arm as Steven grabs me around the waist and helps me regain my feet. My legs have no strength and give way as I slump into Steven's arms. "Get help!" Steven excitedly instructs the foreign aide. She runs to the phone as Steven gently lowers me to the hallway floor.

"What's the matter? Why is he lying down like that?" The nosy broad asks.

"Please step back Dolly." Steven commands her softly. "Mr. Rick will be alright, just go about your business please."

"He's dead." Dolly states as she walks away already having forgotten about me on the floor. It is strangely comfortable here although my head is at an odd angle as I lay on my right shoulder. I think I'll take a nap for a while. I exhale and relax completely.

"Mrs. Scott, the people at Good Samaritan thought your father had a stroke, and it did have many of the characteristics of a stroke. We are not certain what caused him to collapse but did find some disturbing results on the MRI and Cat-scans. Your father is experiencing shrinkage of his brain, and that portion of the brain that controls motor skills is not getting enough blood flow, which probably caused him to faint, lose his balance and fall." The doctor is direct and to the point as he addresses us in the family waiting room of the hospital.

Jeff gently put his hand on my arm, as I ask. "Shrinkage? Can anything be done to the shrinkage?"

"We don't know, but we are recommending some exercises that could stimulate blood flow to his brain to help with the motor skills, and hopefully that will stop the shrinkage as well."

"What if they don't help?"

"We are confident you will see an improvement but of course, can offer no guarantees." The doctor smiled reassuringly, but I suspect he has learned to do that with families.

My mind races, trying to take it all in - shrinkage of the brain - reduced motor skills? "That sounds pretty serious Doctor?"

The doctor studies me for a moment. "Mrs. Scott, it is serious. Is it life threatening?" He nods slowly, averting his gaze from mine, searching for the right words. "It could be, but for certain your father's condition is steadily worsening. I don't want to give you false hope." He pauses, seeking the right words. "Are your father's... affairs in order?"

"Oh!" I gasp. "Are you saying...?" The fear is as obvious on my face as it is in my heart.

"No." He interrupts me, shaking his head. "I am not saying death is imminent but... it is impossible to tell how much longer he may linger on, although... you must realize he is getting close to the end." He pauses, shifting in the chair, he leans back and rests his elbows on the arms of the chair. "His rate of deterioration is much greater than a short time ago. We will order Hospice care to begin at The Good Samaritan; that will help him."

"Hospice? Isn't that what is given to people with... a short time to live?" The fear now fully grips me and Jeff squeezes my arm.

He shakes his head. "That is the general perception, but in truth, many people are released from Hospice because their condition improves to the point they no longer need the additional attention that Hospice offers. Don't be overly concerned or frightened by the term. Some people live for several years after Hospice services are terminated. It is fairly common in these cases and I am sure you will find their services comforting... to you as well as your father."

A hospital style bed has been provided so dad can raise or lower himself in bed, by simply pressing the correct button, to watch television or make it easier to get out of bed. Dolly, of course, thinks it terrible that dad gets to have such a "neat" bed and she does not. Sometimes I'd like to smack her in the face myself. I chuckle at how I want to react to her just as dad once did, and how I scolded him for it. Punched the nosy bitch out! I cannot let on that I am proud of him.

My pride is swallowed as Steven tells me dad is losing control of his bodily functions and how apologetic and embarrassed dad is for messing his bed, and himself. This hurts. Dad is a proud man and having someone clean him up when he cannot control his bowels is... well... I know he hates it.

"Hi dad! How's it goin?" I say as pleasantly as possible leaning over to kiss his forehead. He doesn't answer me and his eyes flit about as if frightened or bewildered. Does he not recognize me? It has only been three days since my last visit and surely he knows who I am.

"It's Dawn daddy."

"Unnh" he grunts, sounding scared as he moves his legs around under the thin blankets on his bed, turning away from me. His cheeks are more sunken and the dark shadows have deepened around his eyes. His hand shakes as he tries to lift it off the bed. Perhaps he is trying not to look at me as he peers toward the windows with the drapes pulled tightly shut. I take his hand and sit on the edge of his bed. His head spins around and looks at me with terror in his eyes. He does not recognize me and fearfully turns toward the window.

"It's Dawn daddy." No acknowledgement. "Have you not been eating well dad?" I ask as his eyes flicker, but do not relocate their focus from the window. His hand lies limply in mine offering no pressure against my grasp. Several quiet minutes pass as I wait for him to acknowledge my presence; finally I release his hand and go in search of Steven.

"Steven. Has my father not been eating?"

"Hi... um... Mrs. Scott, um... well, he has been eating but not well, his appetite has diminished. This morning he was given something to stimulate his appetite, so hopefully that aspect will improve."

"How much weight has he lost? He looks so thin."

"He's lost seventeen pounds since he came back from the hospital, but a lot of that is due to incontinence. He has had several... um episodes... where he lost a great deal of fluids. It is only temporary and he will regain some weight when the incontinence ceases."

I nod, but stammer softly. "He... doesn't seem to know me."

Steven silently surveys the day room full of other patients before returning his gaze to me. "Mr. Rick is very uncomfortable with not being able to control his bowels. He is embarrassed and apologetic when we come to clean him up. He does not like wearing Depends, or diapers as he refers to them. I am sure it is only his embarrassment you saw. He knows you." Steven casts a confident, reassuring smile and I do feel better, although not certain I should believe this young man.

I take dad's hand again as I return to the room but he still does not acknowledge me. It is a quiet visit.

Chapter Seventeen

"Dawn said to prepare ourselves when I talked to her about a month ago." I remind Diane as we near the Good Samaritan Center to see Rick. "She told me Rick has lost a lot of weight, down to one hundred twenty six pounds."

Diane silently nods.

I continue speaking, trying to bolster myself, "He was between one hundred eighty and one hundred ninety pounds for several years before... well... he was too heavy at that weight for his five foot ten inch frame and I used to call him fatso... lovingly of course... I..." I am rambling and finally shut up. We drive in silence for several minutes before we pull into the parking lot.

Dawn is waiting as we park alongside her SUV. We exchange pleasantries, but I avoid her eyes feeling guilty about not having seen my 'brother' for a year.

"Prepare yourself." She begins, "Dad is in a wheelchair, has been for months now, as he can no longer walk. I guess the good news is his ankles are not swollen as much, ha." She laughs nervously. "You are not going to see the same person you have been used to seeing, not even the person you saw the last time you were here."

"I know." I counter, "I have been thinking of little else on the drive down here. That has given me nearly nine hours to ready myself." I laugh nervously, "It has been a pretty quiet trip for Diane as I must admit I was not much into conversation."

Diane smiles as her eyes begin to moisten.

"I can hardly imagine him at one hundred twenty six pounds." I say, shaking my head.

Dawn looks at the ground and whispers, "He's down to one hundred and seven pounds now."

"Oh God." Tears start to fill my eyes and I shake my head in disbelief. "Will he know me?"

"I think so, well… it is impossible to know for sure. He knows me when I come to visit, at least he smiles at me when I come. He doesn't speak much, if at all, he is getting weak, he… ah… forgets to chew his food, to eat properly." She pauses for a couple of moments searching my eyes. "What will it mean to you if he does not recognize you?"

"I have prepared myself for that probability; preparing for the worst, I expect him to not remember me even though we have been very close, almost like brothers, well… you know. Does he ask about me?"

Dawn shakes her head slowly. "No. He has talked about Don." She says softly as if trying not to hurt my feelings. "Sometimes he still talks about Don living in the apartment upstairs." She smiles and we both chuckle. Nothing is said for a few moments until Dawn looks at me and asks. "Ready?"

Dawn has a key allowing direct access to the dimly lit day room. Panning the room and its few occupants, my eyes fall on the emaciated figure sitting in a wheelchair, his back to the far wall, chin drooping nearly to his chest, drool coming from his open lips. Diane draws in her breath sharply and utters a slight moan. Oh jeez! How does one prepare for this! He is almost a living skeleton! His cheeks are sunken and withdrawn, eyes dark and empty. Always the nappy dresser, Rick sits in a wheelchair wearing pajamas, a robe and light blankets thrown over his shoulders and across his legs. Heavy slippers loosely cover his feet. My heart pounds as I force my weak legs to move toward him.

"Who are you?" The old nosy woman I recall from our last visit utters loudly as she approaches us. Her route is intercepted by the young attendant, Steven. I nod toward him as he heads Dolly off and I return my attention to Rick.

Kneeling on the floor in front of him, I take Rick's hands in mine. "How ya doin buddy?" I utter the words lovingly. He looks at me, his eyes flitting back and forth, staring at me, not speaking. "It's Dale, your brother by other parents." I chuckle as I squeeze his hands. He stares blankly at me. Tears come to my eyes as I realize what I had hoped against... he does not know me.

Something is buzzing around my room. The buzzing is loud, then quieter, rapidly changing in intensity as if suddenly approaching and departing very quickly. It also sounds like a clattering sound or clicking. Ah, there it is, I see the shape, a dark very small shape that flies an erratic path around the room. It alights on the ceiling for a moment, walking this way, then that way as if searching for something, then continuing its journey, clicking, clacking, stopping on the wall before landing on my forehead. The staccato buzzing stops and I feel the tickle of the flying object... fly, that's what it is... a fly is walking on my forehead. I slowly lift my hand to pet it but it flies off with the renewed buzzing and clacking sound that accompanies it.

The movements of the fly hold my interest for quite some time as it frequents various parts of my room, stopping occasionally on my cheek, lips or hands. Buzz. The sound grows louder then fainter depending on how near or far the small creature is from me. The rapid change in volume is intriguing as I seek to pick up his movements in the air. At times I see him, but at other times I only hear the buzzing. He does not fly a straight predetermined path, but if he did his location would be predictable and he could be more readily caught. Ah, an erratic path, that is an admirable defense mechanism for this little fella, not being where you think he should be. A quick little bugger, as when I try to catch him, he moves off before I can pet him. I don't want to hurt him as the little fly is the only companion I have seen for some time. What should I name him, or should I name him at all? 'Fly' is my companion, my only friend. He is a good friend. There he is now, walking on the wall near the curtains.

The television set is dark as it rests on a table in the corner of my room. To the left of my bed, just out of reach, are dark curtains with large woven thread. I remember seeing material like this as I walked past the grain elevator in town on my way to school. Trucks and tractors pulling wagons wait their turn to empty their payload at the elevator and receive credit for the crop. Stacked on pallets around the elevator were sacks of grain, the cloth of which is made from a similar type of material that now adorns my windows. My left hand fails to touch the fabric although I strain to reach it. Is there grain still on it? Sniffing the air does not reveal the familiar smell of the grain elevator or its contents.

The elevator was only four blocks from our house and I sometimes stopped in there briefly during the winter to warm up before continuing the remaining ten blocks to school. Even when it got to thirty below zero or more, Dad could not take Don and me to school as he had to work. Dad was a painter and winter was the time he and Uncle Lyle worked inside, when they could get work. He would not disappoint his customers by not showing up on time to work. Sometimes, on really cold days, Don and I would duck into another store for a few minutes as we crossed Main Street, six blocks from school.

'Fly' continues his journey around the room, frequently disappearing for some time before I find him again. There he is. Does he think? If he does, what does he think about? What do I look like to him? I chuckle as I recall the movie "The Fly" and the ten to fifteen images supposedly seen through the eyes of the fly. This one probably thinks I am an old fool not knowing where I am going yet going there in a straight, predictable path. He will find me whenever he wants because he knows where I will be. On the other hand, who can predict where my little friend will be at any given moment? Flies are much smarter than people, although some people can be very devious.

Oh damn! I feel the release of pressure on my stomach and now the squishy feeling under me tells me I have done it again. Damn! I don't want to press the button for... for... well for someone to come and clean me up.

It is not long however, that a dark skinned young man arrives in my room and says pleasantly. "Good afternoon Mr. Rick. Did you have a nice nap? OOH!" He exclaims leaning away from my bedside. "I think you are ready for a shower, OK?"

He steps out for a moment and returns with paper towels and a plastic box with a white colored cloth protruding from the top. Pulling my blanket back, he removes my pajama bottoms, then my shirt and rolls me over to my left side to remove my 'diaper'. The paper towels rub against my skin, sliding gently across my bottom. Each pass with a new set of towels becomes more abrasive than the last, until cloths from the plastic box are put to use in making the final touches in the cleaning process. The cloth is wet and cold and I flinch from the touch.

"Come Mr. Rick. Let's get you into the shower so you will feel better and can come out to the day room with your friends." He says as he pulls my feet over the side of the bed.

"Unnnh." I grunt and point toward the door.

"It's OK Mr. Rick, the door is locked. No one can come in while we take your shower. Your privacy is safe."

I'm not so sure, that nosy old bag keeps trying to get into my room. I wonder if she tries to get into other rooms as well. The bitch, heh heh,… I should just say that to her, 'hey you old bitch, leave me alone!' but that takes too much energy, it will be my little secret… the bitch!

No need to have hurried. I am sitting in my wheelchair with nothing to do and no one to talk to, if I wanted to talk, which I don't. That old bag sitting by the window in a straight backed chair tells me she has children, as if I cared. She's returned her attention to her hands, looking frightened as she stares at her hands gently rubbing against each other. She is overweight, grey haired and wearing glasses. In a blue flower print dress, she looks as my grandmother used to look way back when. So she has children does she, I smile as I recall her comment to me as I was wheeled into the room. Hmmm. I wonder if I do? The grey haired, skinny, nosy bitch, I'll think of her name in a minute, also said she has children. Shut up. Boy would I like to tell them what I think. What do I think? Sometimes I wonder… about… about… I wonder… shit I don't know what I think, or wonder about!

A couple that look to be about my age… how old am I? Oh well, the couple approach an old lady sitting in a wheelchair across the room from me. "Hi Lila. How are you?" The woman coo's.

Suddenly, 'Lila' replies enthusiastically, "Yep! Same as you, same as you."

The man says, "I see you're having lunch Mom."

Looking down 'Lila' replies with a start, "Yep, must be, must be, there's my food, there's my food." She looks at the tray in her lap. The couple find a pair of folding chairs and begin a quiet conversation with the old lady, at least they are quiet, the old lady talks pretty loud.

The day room. That's a silly name for a place so dimly lit. Maybe it should be called the night room, or the dark room. Nah, it is not dark, just dim. It's probably called the day room because we're only in it during the day; at night we are in our own little room where no one can bother us. This room is good for taking naps sitting on the couch, but makes it tougher to keep away from that nosy bitch. To that end it seems like the dark... Steven, that's his name! Phew, thought I would never recall his name. It seems as if Steven spends a great deal of time just getting between the nosy bitch, myself and several of the other people here. He never says much to her, just sort of heads her off from the direction she takes to confront another person.

The day room is a large room about thirty feet square with a hallway emptying into it from my left and beginning again at the far side of the room. Across the way to the other side of the room, a blue colored stuffed chair sits just to the right of the hallway. That chair usually is empty, but is occupied by the old woman talking with a man and a woman who are about my age. The old woman talks much too loud. To the right of the chair is a bookcase with a few neatly placed books and magazines. I study the supporting legs of the bookcase, tracing in my mind the design of the round supports as they separate one shelf from another. Four shelves I count, holding various books I have not bothered to read, come to think of it, I have not seen anyone take a book or magazine to read. That's strange. Why doesn't someone read those books? Maybe I will someday.

To the right of the bookcase is a large radio or something that has small red lights flashing in time to the music that plays. Ah yes, there is music. I have heard that music before, but when? Next is another blue stuffed chair occupied by an old lady that sits staring at her hands, is there something on her hand? I strain my eyes to see but she is fifteen feet away and I cannot make out what she's looking at. Maybe nothing, maybe she is just listening to the music.

Now I remember when I heard that music before. Good music, Dale and I used to play that song on the jukebox at the drive-in restaurant south of town. Many great nights!

That old gal is drooling from her mouth as she sits and stares at her lap or hands. God she is old!

To the right of that old lady is a narrow table with flowers on it that may or may not be real, can't tell from here. Not that it matters, I could care less about flowers, flowers are for sissies and I am not a sissy. The table and flowers front a large window covered with drapes that allow only a small amount of sunlight in. The curtains are slightly open and I strain to see what, if anything, is going on outside. Outside... how long have I been inside? When was the last time I was outside? That is a good question, I wonder about the outside, what is out there? Is it warm or cold out there? It's not... oh what is it called... when it is, when there are... there are... puddles, wet... wet... it looks like rain falling, oh yeah, rain, that's it, rain. Well it must not be raining now as it does look relatively bright outside and it has to be dark... doesn't it... for rain to happen?

The old lady sitting to the right of the window notices me as my gaze reaches her again and she says. "I have children. I have five boys and..."

"I have more." I hear to my left and turn slowly to see the old nosy bitch being redirected by... by... oh yeah, by Steven, as he says, "That's great Dolly." Dolly. That's the nosy bitch's name? Dolly, I'll have to remember that. I smile and snicker to myself, why would I want to remember that nosy bitch's name? Sometimes it's good not to be able to remember stuff.

"Mmmmph." I am surprised at the mumble coming from my lips. I had not intended to say anything and really didn't, I guess, as surely a mumble cannot mean I spoke.

Steven has successfully directed the nosy bitch's attention elsewhere, but follows behind as she walks around the room spouting her opinion about one thing or another, or everything, who listens? The center of the dayroom is open and currently being used by... that nosy bitch, to wander about in. Damn, I just had her name a minute ago! Oh well, nosy bitch will suffice. I return my attention to studying the rest of the dayroom.

I wonder what is behind the wheelchair I sit in; there is a large television to the right of me, but what is behind me? I slowly turn my head but too much effort is required for me to look behind me, I will have to stand up and turn around. I'll look when I stand up again. Can I stand, move this chair by myself? Somehow my hands do not respond, although I want to move the chair.

To my left is a table with an unlit lamp upon it. I am startled to see an old lady sitting in a wheelchair close to my left and between the table with the lamp and another couch perpendicular to us. Her eyes are closed, in sleep I suspect. She is the oldest of the five of us, I think. Maybe she's dead, nah, what's his name would do something about it if she were.

Completing my sweep of the dayroom, I return my gaze to the starting point, the hallway and the wall adjacent to it. The passageway leading to the left, where does that go? Is that a kitchen I see through a doorway in the wall? Where is it we have our meals? What is behind that wall? I see a desk to the left of the hallway next to the chair where... that's the hallway leading to my room! Seated at the desk is a female attendant with a small lamp lighting the work she busily performs. Her head moves back and forth as she scans the ledger, or whatever it is that holds her fascination. There is a corridor to her left. Is that connected to the kitchen I see through a door on the wall to my left?

Steven asks the nosy bitch to sit on the couch. "Dolly... everyone? Would you like me to read to you?" Is he waiting for a response? If so he will have a long wait as there is only one of us with an inclination to speak. Steven goes to the bookcase and eyes several volumes before pulling one out. Studying them momentarily, he lifts his head and surveys his "audience". Only the nosy bitch makes any motion as she leaves the couch and is intercepted by Steven who directs her back to the couch where she takes her seat. No one else seems to notice, or care, about what Steven does.

He opens the book and motions for Dolly to remain seated as he scans the room. "This is the book on poetry we started yesterday, I will read a couple of poems at random." He directs his attention to the pages and turns them slowly as his eyes scan up and down. "OK, this one looks good. It is by Thomas Hardy." Steven draws a deep breath and begins to read.

"Your Last Drive.
'Here by the moorway you returned,
and saw the burrough lights ahead
That lit your face – all undiscerned

To be in a week the face of the…' "OH! OH! Well, maybe I'll choose something else." and returns to flipping through the pages. He stops and studies the page for a moment, then turns another page that he also studies. "Here! Here is one by William Butler Yeats called 'To the Rose upon the Rood of Time'

'Red Rose, proud Rose, sad Rose of all my days!
Come near me, while I sing the ancient ways:
Cuhoolin battling with the bitter tide;'

"I used Tide!" Dolly interrupts as she jumps off the couch.

"I have children." The old lady by the window chimes in.

Steven gently assists Dolly back to her place on the couch and continues.

'Cuhoolin battling with the bitter... ' He allows his voice to tail off as he looks at Dolly and does not repeat tide.

'The Druid, gray, wood nurtured, quiet-eyed,
Who cast round Fergus dreams, and ruin untold,
And thine own sadness, whereof stars, grown old
In dancing silver sandalled on the sea,
Sing in their high and lonely melody.
Come near, that no more blinded by man's fate,
I find under the boughs of love and hate,
In all poor foolish things that live a day,
Eternal Beauty wandering on her way.
Come near, come near, come near – Ah, leave me still.'

"Dolly, please be seated. Don't you want to hear the rest of the poem?"

Dolly is having none of it as she is heading for the hallway. Steven quickly closes the book and starts after her. Returning Dolly to the couch, the young man picks up the book and returns it to the bookcase. Damn! What he was reading about?

'Fly' is buzzing around again, but seems to be flying in a straight line. No, don't do that! They'll get you! Look out little buddy! Look out little Fly! I want to scream a warning but... Where is he? I hear him, but do not see him. Buzz. He must be close by, I can hear him plainly. Dolly waves her hand in the air as if trying to catch something. Not my friend? Leave him alone I scream silently.

There he goes again, louder, quieter, then louder again before stopping suddenly on my cheek. Ah, there you are my friend. He has come to me for comfort. Yes, stay here my friend, stay by me. He crawls on my ear. Keep me company, I smile. No! Don't go! He is off again.

Steven comes out of the kitchen holding a wire stick with a flat piece of rubber on the end and looks about the room. What is he doing? The buzzing stops over my head and Steven stealthily approaches looking intently over my head. Slowly he raises the wire stick and swings it quickly against the wall over my head. "Got it!" He exclaims.

Got it? What did he get? Steven pushes my chair forward a couple of feet and reaches down to the floor. Holding a dark shape between his fingers he proudly proclaims, "This fly won't bother you any more Mr. Rick."

This fly? Did he… surely he didn't… 'Fly'… my friend, my only friend? NO!

My head begins to ache. The ringing in my ears intensifies and my arms are heavy. A fog encroaches on my senses, a burning sensation rises in my throat and arms, a heavy tightness, a great pain and pounding in my chest that suddenly stops. My breath sounds as if it is coming from inside a hollow shell, suddenly I can't hear my breathing. Is that dark skinned boy yelling at me? His lips are moving, but he makes no sound. He is rushing toward me looking concerned. A grey circle invades the periphery of my sight and the room gets fuzzy, fading into a darkness, the grey circles closing in, my vision fading, becoming less clear as if... as if...

I didn't think she'd be here. That bitch Angel never cared about dad when he was alive and now... oh well. Try to be nice to the bitch, soon you won't have to see her ever again. Dad's brother Don and his sisters came from Minnesota, but grandma had a heart attack when she heard of dad's death and now there have been two deaths in the family, two funerals to attend. Dale and Diane came from Kansas City, Dave from San Antonio, but only a few of dad's friends from Plano came to the simple ceremony prior to the cremation. Here comes Angel, be nice.

"I'm so sorry Dawn..."

"Got what you wanted bitch?" Damn! Couldn't hold my tongue, just had to say what I thought. She is getting dads' house and has already taken most of his money, the greedy bitch. She'll get hers someday.

Chapter Eighteen

This room looks familiar. I have been here before. It looks a lot like my bedroom, although the bed and its' coverings are different. Has someone taken my bedding and thrown it away? The television that has been sitting against the wall to my left, whoa wait a minute… that is not my television. My television is not mounted on the wall, and is not so thin. What the hell? Beyond the television is the short hallway leading to the remainder of the house.

The couch I am sitting on… Whoa! HOLY SHIT! Where are my feet? What happened to my feet? I can't see my feet although I can feel them dangling over the side of the couch. Wait… dangling? Why are my feet not touching the floor? I am sitting on a couch, my feet should be touching the floor, what the hell is going on?

As I move effortlessly around the room, I peer into my bathroom, yes… it is my bathroom but a different color. How did that happen? Who painted it pink? I don't like pink, I would never paint it pink. That's sissy colors! Oh jeez! A towel is thrown limply over the top of the shower door and I see clothing on the edge of the bathtub. Wow, I must be getting sloppy, must pick them up as soon as I can.

I don't recognize the picture on the wall, it was not there before… and who painted the damn walls dark red? I like white or soft colors, why are my walls red?

Through the door of the short hallway strides Angel, or at least it looks like Angel, but much older. This Angel has grey hair and looks to be in her fifties, maybe sixties. She is also much heavier, very wide at the hips. How can this be, how can Kay's daughter look so old all of a sudden?

"AHHHHHYYEEEAH!" Angel stops and throws herself against the wall as she stares at me. "AAAAYEEEEH! AAAAEEEHHH!" She continues to scream. What the hell is wrong with that bitch?

Chase runs into the bedroom, "Angel! What is it? What's wrong?"

Damn, he's old too! He has lost most of his hair and what he has is grey. His football player physique has been replaced by a large pot belly. He has to be over three hundred pounds, no, more than that... three fifty?

Angel points at me, the terror clearly evident in her eyes.

"What?" Chase asks, "What?"

"WHAT?" Angel screams, turning her head slightly and angrily addressing her husband, "There. That is what, those things on the couch, that's what!"

Chase stares at me a moment then looks at Angel again. Coming closer he stares again at me, but turns to Angel, "What are you talking about? There is nothing there."

"ON THE GODDAMN COUCH DAMN YOU! ON THE COUCH! THREE OF THEM, DAMN YOU"

I look to my left and... damned if she isn't right, there are three of us sitting here. I don't recognize the

198

others but they don't have feet either. Whoa, wait a minute! Chase can't see us? Only Angel can see us? No feet? I remember when only I could see… wait a minute.

I lean back and smile. Oh boy, this is going to be fun! Payback! Ha ha ha ha ha ha ha!

Made in the USA
Middletown, DE
04 August 2020